# UN PEACEKEEPING

## JAPANESE AND AMERICAN PERSPECTIVES

EDITED BY

### SELIG S. HARRISON
CARNEGIE ENDOWMENT FOR INTERNATIONAL PEACE

### MASASHI NISHIHARA
RESEARCH INSTITUTE FOR PEACE AND SECURITY

A CARNEGIE ENDOWMENT BOOK

*U.N. Peacekeeping: Japanese and American Perspectives* can be ordered from the Brookings Institution, Department 029, Washington, D.C. 20041-0029. USA Tel. 1/800/275-1447 (except Washington, D.C. 202-797-6258). Fax 202-797-6004.

*Edited by Jennifer Collins Stanley.*
*Design by Paddy McLaughlin, Concepts & Design.*
*Photos: Front cover top—Junji Kurokawa/Agence France Presse;*
*middle and bottom—P.S. Sudhakaran/United Nations.*
*Back cover—Kazuhiro Nogi/Agence France Presse.*
*Printed by Automated Graphic Systems.*

*Library of Congress Cataloging-in-Publication Data*

United Nations peacekeeping: Japanese and American perspectives/
edited by: Selig S. Harrison, Masashi Nishihara
192 pp. 15x22.5 cms.
ISBN: 0-87003-066-3
1. United Nations—Armed Forces   2. United Nations—United States
3. United Nations—Japan
I. Harrison, Selig S. II. Nishihara, Masashi
JX1981.P7U414 1995
327.1'72—dc20'                                         95-24562
                                                       CIP

# CONTENTS

# FOREWORD

For the past four decades, the United Nations has played a significant peacekeeping role with the consent of the warring parties in Cyprus, the Golan Heights, the Congo and other flashpoints of conflict. During the Cold War, however, the superpower rivalry often paralyzed the Security Council, severely limiting what the United Nations could do in many crises. The passing of the Cold War has now prompted unprecedented efforts to redefine and broaden the U.N. role to embrace peace enforcement with or without the consent of the antagonists, often in combination with traditional peacekeeping.

The widespread controversy generated by the American-supported expansion of the peacekeeping concept has been particularly acute in Japan. Political leaders in Tokyo who advocate a more activist Japanese global role have been pressing for Japanese participation in U.N. peacekeeping in partnership with Washington as an extension of the Japan–U.S. Security Treaty. Opponents of Japanese involvement in peacekeeping have warned that approval of a combat role for Japan in U.N. operations would lead to pressures for more wide-ranging military adventures abroad. The Japanese Diet reached a compromise in 1992 that made possible the subsequent assignment of non-combat Japanese Self-Defense Force units to Cambodia, Zaire, and Mozambique. But the nature and extent of Japanese participation in U.N. peacekeeping is still a subject of intense controversy.

The Carnegie Endowment for International Peace and the Research Institute for Peace and Security decided to conduct a joint American-Japanese examination of "U.N. Peacekeeping: Japanese and American Perspectives" with two principal objectives: first, to promote dialogue between specialists in the two countries on the role that the United Nations should play in maintaining world order and the criteria that should govern U.N. involvement in future conflicts; and second, to explore the possibilities for cooperation between the two countries in U.N. peacekeeping as an adjunct to the U.S.–Japan security partnership. Twelve Japanese and American specialists met for a two-day discussion in Yokohama on May 17 and 18, 1994. This volume presents the eight papers prepared for the conference in the belief that they will enrich the ongoing debate in the two countries on the U.N.'s future.

The co-sponsors would like to express appreciation to the U.S. Institute of Peace for making the publication of this book possible and to the Japan Foundation–Center for Global Partnership for supporting the Yokohama Conference and publication of a companion edition in Japanese.

**Selig S. Harrison**
**Masashi Nishihara**

# SELIG S. HARRISON | OVERVIEW

n June 15, 1992, climaxing a bitter, two-year parliamentary stalemate, the Japanese Diet authorized sharply circumscribed Japanese participation in U.N. peacekeeping missions. The sticking point in the protracted Diet debate was Article 9 of the Japanese Constitution, which renounces war "as a sovereign right of the nation, and the threat or use of force as a means of settling international disputes." Warning against a backdoor effort to revive militarism, opposition Diet members had forced the government to accept a legislative compromise limiting Japanese forces to a non-combat peacekeeping role. Self-Defense Force units could go abroad in U.N. missions, but they would be restricted to specified categories of logistic support and humanitarian activity, such as construction, supervising elections, and medical care. They were explicitly barred from peacekeeping functions normally performed by U.N. forces, including monitoring ceasefire agreements, patrolling buffer zones, and disarming hostile forces.

It was just two days after this halting Japanese step toward support of the traditional U.N. peacekeeping role that Secretary-General Boutros Boutros-Ghali made his controversial proposal on June 17 for a much more ambitious U.N. peace enforcement concept. With a bluntness uncharacteristic in Japanese foreign policy pronouncements, Foreign Minister Michio Watanabe peremptorily dismissed the proposal soon thereafter in his maiden address to the General Assembly. Watanabe declared that "Japan believes the principles and practices of peacekeeping operations upheld by the United Nations for more than forty years are still both appropriate and valid today, and will continue to be so in the future."

When the Clinton Administration embraced the concept of peace enforcement in early 1993, the gulf between Japanese and American perspectives on the U.N. role appeared unbridgeable. American spokesmen confidently advocated what U.N. Representative Madeleine Albright called an "assertive multilateralism." As John Isaacs points out in Section II of this book, however, "Administration officials and many in Europe began to use the United Nations as a scapegoat for their own policy failures" in Somalia and above all in Bosnia, where they "gave the United Nations an expansive mandate to solve problems—but without providing the resources . . . or political backing to fulfill the job."

By 1994, as disenchantment with the United Nations took hold in the United States, the gap between American and Japanese

3

thinking began to narrow. President Clinton had issued Presidential Decision Directive 25, severely curbing U.S. participation in U.N. operations. Republican leaders vowed to enact legislation that would bar U.S. forces from serving under foreign commanders, which would "make it difficult, if not impossible," as *The Washington Post* observed, "for the President to commit US troops to new or expanded UN operations or even to continue support for ongoing activities." On the fiftieth anniversary of the United Nations, two of its most influential congressional supporters, Lee Hamilton (D-IN) and Nancy Landon Kassebaum (R-KS), declared that "peacekeeping is diplomacy with light arms. It is not designed to fight wars. We believe that 'peace enforcement' should be struck from the UN's vocabulary and that future peacekeeping should be limited to classic operations in which 'Blue Helmets' stand between suspicious parties only after diplomacy has secured a peace to be kept."

The essays presented in this book reflect significant differences in emphasis but a broad consensus in support of an active U.N. role in preventive diplomacy, peacemaking, and peacekeeping, coupled with a reappraisal of peace enforcement designed to avoid a repetition of the mistakes made in Somalia and Bosnia.

**Steven Ratner** and **Masahiko Asada** lay the foundations for the essays to follow with their analysis of the conceptual and legal underpinnings of the U.N. role in preserving international order.

Ratner analyzes the distinctions between peacemaking, exemplified by the successful U.N. mediation effort in Afghanistan that led to the Soviet withdrawal; "first-generation" peacekeeping, limited to freezing conflicts in place pending a political settlement, as in Cyprus and the Golan Heights; "second-generation" peacekeeping, designed to implement the political solution of an interstate or internal conflict, such as the U.N. role in Cambodia; and peace enforcement. Even before the advent of peace enforcement, he observes, "second-generation" peacekeeping had tarnished the image of the United Nations as an impartial umpire because it had "intruded the United Nations into the implementation of political settlements in a way that inevitably affects the relative power of the belligerents." The United Nations, he concludes, "faces a core dilemma: If it relies heavily upon mediation to resolve disputes, the parties may regard it as weak; if it attempts to push forward a peace plan through more assertive means, the recalcitrant parties may regard it as biased. This quandary becomes even more severe if an operation combines mandates of peacekeeping, with its requirement of impartiality, and peace enforcement, which lacks any such stricture, as occurred in the Somalia and Yugoslavia missions in 1993 and 1994."

Asada delivers a harsh verdict with respect to the peace-enforcement concept. With the sole exception of the Congo in 1961, he points out, the Security Council had never authorized U.N. troops to use force for purposes other than their own self-defense until the case of Somalia in 1993. He emphasizes that the late Secretary-General Ralph Bunche actually used force in the Congo only to evacuate foreign troops and mercenaries. "While, in Somalia, U.N. military might has been directed against the Somali people themselves," he writes, Bunche "declined the U.S. proposal to attack the Congolese National Army, his aim being always to avoid a situation in which U.N. soldiers might be forced to shoot at the Congolese."

It was a "revolutionary" departure, he observes, when the Security Council accepted Boutros-Ghali's recommendation in March 1993 that U.N. forces in Somalia should be endowed with enforcement powers under Chapter VII of the Charter in order to disarm the clans. Similarly, in Bosnia, the Council authorized the use of force not only to defend U.N. forces themselves but also to retaliate in the event of bombardments against the "safe areas," armed incursions into these areas, and the obstruction of "protected humanitarian convoys." Asada describes both Somalia and Bosnia as essentially "civil war–type situations . . . [in which] enforcement activities have targeted some particular group in each country," thus compromising the principle of impartiality on which the acceptance of U.N. intervention rests. In his view, attempting to combine peacekeeping with peace enforcement "will almost inevitably amount to an awkward half-measure" that will "prove fruitless at the end of the day; or worse . . . may aggravate the situation." In order to restore and maintain its credibility, he concludes, the United Nations should adopt a "selective approach" to future conflicts, "considering in particular the aptitude and capabilities of the United Nations in peacekeeping for dealing with the given conflict and whether the parties concerned have the intention and ability themselves to settle the dispute."

**W**hile stopping short of explicit prophecy, **John Isaacs** and **Akihiko Tanaka,** analyzing attitudes toward peacekeeping in the United States and Japan, foresee strong resistance to the peace-enforcement concept and continued debate over whether to support any peacekeeping at all, with little prospect that Japan will send combat forces on peacekeeping missions.

In the United States, Isaacs believes, the immediate issue in the years ahead will be how much support Congress will give to traditional peacekeeping missions, which now receive 30 percent of their financing from Washington. While Congress claims to reflect public opinion, he finds a disconnect between congressional antagonism to the United Nations, especially on the part of the Republican majority, and public opinion research that shows substantial support for peacekeeping. Among a wide range of studies, he cites a 1994 *New York Times* poll in which those questioned agreed by a 59 to 31 percent margin that the United States "has a responsibility to contribute military support to enforce peace plans in trouble spots around the world when it is asked by the UN." Criticizing the "confusion and indecision" of the Clinton Administration, Isaacs concludes that "determined" leadership by the White House could reverse the anti–U.N. tide.

In the case of Japan, Tanaka shows how difficult it was for supporters of a Japanese peacekeeping role to push through the 1992 legislative compromise. But he expects the compromise to stick. Domestic political support for peacekeeping has increased, he notes, as a result of the positive image of the Japanese role in Cambodia and the reversal of Socialist opposition to the use of the Self-Defense Forces in U.N. missions during the tenure of Socialist Tomiichi Murayama as Prime Minister. What is still questionable is whether a Diet majority will at some point permit Japanese forces to perform the combat and quasi-combat functions that have long been central to traditional peacekeeping. In an April 1994 poll, 33 percent of those questioned favored a removal of the 1992 restrictions on a combat role, but 50 percent were opposed. Most Japanese political prophets were predicting in mid-1994 that none of the most likely successors to Murayama are likely to endorse a removal of these restrictions and that the strongest advocate of a combat role, Ichiro Ozawa, leader of the Renewal Party, is not likely to assume the Prime Ministership in the foreseeable future.

Significantly, in imposing its restrictions in 1992, the Diet did not bar Japanese forces from a combat role in perpetuity. Instead, it imposed a three-year, renewable "freeze" barring the performance of six specified peacekeeping functions by Japanese forces pending further review. Tanaka judges it to be "problematic . . . whether and to what extent Japan will do more in U.N. peace operations." With a note of impatience, he asks: "If, as Michio Watanabe said at the United Nations in 1993, the principles of U.N. peacekeeping are still appropriate and valid, why does Japan continue to 'freeze' the most important elements of traditional peacekeeping?" Such a position, he warns, may not be compatible with Japan's effort to win a permanent seat in the U.N. Security Council.

One of the pervasive themes running through all of the essays in this book in greater or lesser degree is the need for preventive diplomacy to keep conflicts from escalating to unmanageable levels of violence. **Edward C. Luck** and **Takako Ueta** discuss specific institutional approaches to conflict resolution in the context of a broader examination of the possibility of shifting peacekeeping efforts to the regional level.

As Luck reminds us, the U.N. Charter specifically said that disputants should first seek to resolve conflicts through any "regional arrangements" and "regional agencies" available before turning to the Security Council. But in the case of East Asia, he observes, no "regional arrangements" for conflict resolution yet exist. Moreover, since Russia and China have Security Council vetoes, the Council itself could well be immobilized in any East Asian crisis involving Moscow or Beijing. For this reason, he argues, the Japan–U.S. Security Treaty remains critical to regional stability. The unraveling of the treaty, Luck says, would not only destabilize relations among the United States, Japan, China, and Russia, but could also "lead to a more pacifist or a more militarist Japan"— neither of which is in his view "a desirable outcome in terms of international stability or Japanese domestic tranquility."

While urging continuance of the treaty, however, he calls for parallel movement toward regional security arrangements, starting with quadrilateral exchanges between Washington, Tokyo, Moscow, and Beijing, possibly leading to the establishment of a four-way "hot line." This should set the stage for launching a permanent forum for dialogue designed to increase transparency and prevent conflicts. He questions the workability of proposals to deal with security issues within the framework of existing regional groupings addressed primarily to economic goals, such as the Asia-Pacific Economic Cooperation forum and the Association of South-East Asian Nations (ASEAN) Regional Forum. A more effective approach, he suggests, would be an organization on security and cooperation in Asia patterned after the Organization on Security and Cooperation in Europe (OSCE).

Takako Ueta singles out the OSCE as a model for regional approaches to peacekeeping. Given the fact that it focuses on preventive diplomacy and disavows any peace-enforcement role, she says, Japan can comfortably cooperate with it. Moreover, since the OSCE area of jurisdiction "surrounds" Japan, reaching as it does "from San Francisco to Vladivostok," she argues that it is necessary for Japan to be involved in its affairs "in order to defend its vital security interests." Japan may have a role to play in OSCE affairs not only in preventive diplomacy and crisis management, she suggests, but also in humanitarian assistance and disaster relief operations.

Like Luck, Ueta favors the development of a regional security forum in Asia to promote transparency and confidence-building measures but sees little prospect of the emergence of a regional organization strong enough to carry out peacekeeping functions. It is the United Nations that would have to intervene in any regional security crisis, she declares. The only specific contingency that she mentions is one involving a North Korean nuclear capability, which would not be exclusively a regional crisis but "an issue of proliferation and global concern." While American and Japanese military assets could be utilized in support of a U.N. operation in Korea, she concludes, "the Japan–U.S. Security Treaty itself is not a framework for peacekeeping . . . In contrast with NATO, there seems to be less of a rationale to add a peacekeeping mission to the Japan–U.S. military alliance in order to prolong its life."

**W**illiam Durch gives greater emphasis than any other author to the roots of conflict in the poverty and economic inequities that often underlie social tensions. He calls for preventive economic measures in the form of multilateral and bilateral development and humanitarian assistance, which should be presented to skeptical electorates, in his view, as "a long-term investment in international stability." When political and social tensions in a country reach the danger point, he writes, the international community should then give a much higher priority than in the past to preventive diplomacy and peacemaking efforts. Finally, when preventive efforts fail and conflicts erupt, the United Nations should intervene militarily only in selected cases, and member states should not support peacekeeping indiscriminately.

"It is vitally important," he maintains, "that a government convince itself that significant national interests are bound up with participation in a U.N. operation, especially one that entails some military risk." As examples of the specific circumstances that are likely to determine whether the international community intervenes in a given case, he cites the size of the country involved; operational feasibility; "the severity of the event;" and how the conflict affects the "traditional national economic and balance-of-power interests of the would-be intervenors (for example, access to energy sources or to the sea . . . ). The larger the target country, the more remote from the sea, the less acute the event, and the poorer the fit with traditional interests, the less likely will be international military intervention."

In cases where the United Nations does intervene militarily, Durch suggests that Japan could make an important contribution by helping to meet airlift needs. Currently, he points out, the United States, Russia, and Ukraine are the only countries capable of carrying out heavy airlift operations. But he notes that Japan is considering the acquisition of such capabilities, citing the 1994 *Report of the Prime Minister's Advisory Group on Defense Issues*. "From the viewpoint of participating in U.N. peacekeeping operations and other international activities," said the Advisory Group, "we believe it will be necessary to build a certain degree of long-haul transport capability."

"Were Japan to acquire long-range aircraft capability," Durch concludes, "it would be able to complement U.S. airlift capabilities, in particular, and operate as a full partner in the deployment of U.N. peace operations globally." Since the United States is now replacing its aging, narrow-bodied C-141 aircraft with wide-bodied C-17s, if Japan were to purchase C-17s, "it could function on an interoperable basis with the United States. Concerns about the appearance of a prohibited military power projection capability might be reduced by permanently detailing these aircraft to a standing International Peace Cooperation Corps headquarters; by pre-designating them for U.N. callup; by making them available secondarily for domestic and regional disaster relief operations, and by relying on American in-flight refueling capacity for long-range deployments."

**M**asashi Nishihara also focuses on the importance of improving airlift capabilities as the key to Japanese-American cooperation in supporting U.N. peacekeeping. However, he stops short of recommending the acquisition of new aircraft to supplement the 15 C-130s now available to the Self-Defense Forces. Instead, he calls for emergency laws empowering the Japanese government to commandeer private aircraft and ships in the event of crisis. During the Gulf War, he recalls, labor union opposition prevented the Japanese government from providing commercial aircraft to help transport U.S. troops and equipment to the Middle East.

While Nishihara believes that the Japanese public "may be slow" in accepting a combat role for U.N. peacekeepers, he suggests that the mood could quickly change. For example, he asks how the Japanese public would react if Japanese peacekeepers in Zaire, armed only with sidearms and one light machine gun each, were to be attacked by Zairean troops or Rwandan refugees. He foresees a possible change in attitudes if the public should conclude that a continued taboo on combat forces in U.N. peacekeeping missions is incompatible with Security Council membership. One of the determining factors in the peacekeeping debate underlined in his analysis is whether or not Ichiro Ozawa will emerge from the political power struggles ahead with increased influence. Ozawa not only supports "unfreezing" the restriction on combat but also the establishment of a Japanese U.N. Reserve Force, distinct from the Self-Defense Forces, for "deployment in response to U.N. requests and under U.N. command."

As an example of what Japan and the United States could do together if Japanese policy changes, Nishihara proposes the establishment of a U.N. naval and air peacekeeping force—with Japanese and American forces at its "core"—to monitor the movement of ships and aircraft in the South China Sea. If China should veto such a force, he advocates the creation of a regional peacekeeping force without Chinese approval in which Japanese and U.S. forces would serve as the "major components," if possible with the blessing of the ASEAN Post-Ministerial Conference.

Nishihara makes clear that "unfreezing" the restrictions on combat forces would not imply Japanese readiness to participate in peace-enforcement operations. What it would do is enable Japan to perform traditional peacekeeping functions. He expresses strong disapproval of the confusion in U.S. policy that led to punitive air strikes against Bosnian Serb positions at a time when U.N. peacekeepers were exposed to danger from these strikes in the target areas. "Japanese troops would not be placed in that kind of situation," he concludes. "Restrained Japanese peacekeepers and American peace enforcers can hardly work together."

There is no clear consensus in these essays on the most difficult issues that will confront the international community in establishing the criteria that should govern the future U.N. peacekeeping role:

- Should the United Nations intervene in civil wars?
- If so, should such intervention stop short of peace enforcement, as in the case of Namibia, El Salvador, Cambodia, and Mozambique?
- Or should the United Nations continue to pursue peace enforcement, but with the application of adequate force?
- How should a civil war be defined?

Asada treats both Somalia and Bosnia as essentially "civil war–type situations." In the case of Somalia, few, if any, observers would dissent. It is generally recognized that the disorder leading to U.N. intervention resulted from the internecine power struggles of a society that had never historically achieved enduring nationhood. Postmortems on the lessons learned in Somalia, while differing on many issues, largely agree that the United Nations compromised its ability to function effectively there by taking sides politically and militarily in these struggles. By contrast, in the former Yugoslavia, the crux of the controversy over what the United States and the United Nations should do has been whether Bosnia-Herzegovina should be treated as an established state subject to external attack by Serbia, in alliance with the Bosnian Serbs, or as one of the contenders in an unresolved domestic struggle over how to redistribute power and territory in a dismembered state.

Bosnian Muslim and Croat political leaders declared Bosnia-Herzegovina to be a sovereign state in October 1991. By any objective standard, the conflict that resulted was a textbook example of a civil war because the Bosnian Serbs, who constitute 31 percent of the population, had made clear their unwillingness to be part of the new state; had declared their intention to challenge it militarily; and had served notice that they would seek a federated relationship with Serbia or absorption into a Greater Serbia. If the Bosnian Muslims and Croats could secede from Yugoslavia to escape the domination of Serbia, the Bosnian Serbs said, they were entitled to secede from the new state to escape Muslim and Croat domination.

It is not germane here to consider the factors that governed the U.S. decision to recognize the new state on April 7, 1992, to assess the policies subsequently pursued by two U.S. administrations, or to pass judgment on the morality of the methods used by the Serb forces to achieve their goals. What is relevant is the distinction between the right of the United States and its allies to pursue their own objectives in a situation of this character and the more limited role that the United Nations can play as an international organization embracing divergent views.

Once the United States had taken the fateful step of recognition, it followed logically for many observers in the United States, Europe, and elsewhere to argue that Serbia should be treated as an aggressor; to dismiss peacemaking initiatives like the Vance-Owen plan as appeasement; and to call for intervention on the side of Bosnia. But the United Nations, by its nature, was consigned to impartiality in what was regarded by many of its member states as an "essentially civil war–type situation." Although the new state was seated in the General Assembly on May 22, it is noteworthy that in June 1993, when the Security Council assigned the United Nations to defend designated "safe areas," only 87 out of 184 U.N. member states had joined the United States in extending recognition to the new state. In July 1995, 96 countries had recognized the Sarajevo regime.

This was not a case like Korea or the Gulf War in which established international boundaries had been violated. The "Uniting for Peace" resolution on November 3, 1950, which gave General Assembly sanction to the U.N. role in Korea, was approved overwhelmingly by a 47 to 5 vote. In Bosnia, the United Nations intervened nominally to play a critically needed humanitarian role in the face of horrendous human suffering. In seeking to mitigate this suffering, however, the Security Council shaped the role of the United Nations in a way that not only compromised its impartial status but also was blind to realities. As Asada emphasizes, creating the "safe areas" without Serb concurrence and then assigning U.N.

peacekeepers to retaliate in the event of armed incursions into these areas was indeed a "revolutionary" departure from past U.N. practice. Since these were not to be demilitarized zones, and Bosnian Muslim forces entrenched in these sanctuaries were free to retain their weapons, the Serbs predictably viewed them as enemy fortresses. Moreover, as Isaacs observes, committing the U.N. forces to the defense of the "safe areas" without giving the U.N. forces adequate military capabilities set the stage for predictable military debacles that have gravely weakened the credibility of the United Nations.

The hard reality underlined by recent experiments in peace enforcement is that the United Nations can only make an effective humanitarian or peacekeeping contribution to the extent accepted by the contending parties. Despite this built-in limitation, however, there is great scope for an expanding U.N. role in a world alive with ethnic conflict, territorial disputes, and the social tensions that accompany economic inequities. As Durch emphasizes, there is an urgent need, in particular, for the member states to strengthen the new Department of Humanitarian Affairs and other U.N. capabilities charged with addressing humanitarian crises. One among the many tragic legacies of Somalia and Bosnia is that the United Nations has suffered a loss of credibility at precisely the moment in history when it is most needed. But the damage need not prove irreparable, these essays suggest, if the United Nations rededicates itself to preventive diplomacy and returns to the peacekeeping principles that have guided it for four decades, insisting above all that the member states provide the economic and military resources necessary for success before it crosses the Rubicon of intervention.

# PEACEMAKING, PEACEKEEPING, AND PEACE ENFORCEMENT:

## CONCEPTUAL AND LEGAL UNDERPINNINGS OF THE U.N. ROLE

The past five decades have witnessed the evolution of a variety of different powers and processes by the United Nations—on the part of both its member states and the secretariat—to fulfill the Organization's primary goal of maintaining international peace and security. These undertakings have taken the form of both diplomatic activity and executive action.

On the diplomatic front, the term **peacemaking** has come to be understood as diplomatic action by the organs of the United Nations to bring the parties to a dispute toward a settlement. Typically under the leadership of the Secretary-General, though often with the support of the General Assembly and the Security Council through resolutions and otherwise, the United Nations becomes a mediator, a forum for good offices, or a conciliator in attempting to move the parties toward agreement. Peacemaking does not engage the United Nations in imposing any particular solution upon the parties through use of military force, though it could entail economic sanctions.

**Peacekeeping** is a far more complex phenomenon. During the U.N.'s first forty years, participants in and observers of the United Nations seemed to agree on peacekeeping's definition and essential attributes—the stationing of U.N. military personnel, with the consent of warring states, to monitor ceasefires and dissuade violations through interposition between armies, pending a political settlement. This definition has covered operations in the Sinai, Kashmir, Lebanon, Yemen, Cyprus, and the Golan Heights. Apart from unusual cases in the Congo and western New Guinea, none succeeded in more than freezing conflicts in place, although that itself represented a feat given the tension between the belligerents. Indeed, the U.N. presence may well have prolonged the underlying conflict by removing incentives to settle it.

Since 1989, the United Nations has authorized or deployed a host of new missions still popularly called peacekeeping operations, as well as several smaller monitoring and assistance missions. In Latin America, these have included Haiti (one in 1990 and two in 1993), Nicaragua, El Salvador, and Guatemala; in Africa,

Namibia, Angola (in 1989–1991 and 1991 to the present), Western Sahara, Somalia (in 1992–93 and 1993 to the present), Mozambique, South Africa, Eritrea, Uganda-Rwanda, Liberia, and Rwanda (1993–94 and 1994 to the present); in Europe, the former Yugoslavia, and Georgia. To these must be added one in the Persian Gulf area and two in Cambodia (in 1991–92 and 1992–93). Nearly all of these missions had, in various ways, novel mandates compared with the pre-1989 group.

This new form of peacekeeping emerged as a response to certain new realities caused by the end of the Cold War—the solution of several U.S.–Soviet proxy wars and other conflicts on the agenda of the developing world; the increase in intra-state violence (often ethnically based conflict); the forceful and more balanced assertion by the West of its doctrinal commitment to political and civil rights and democracy; and the cooperation among the great powers in response to Iraq's invasion of Kuwait. These trends led the United Nations to alter the targets and instrumental purposes of peacekeeping.

The result was the emergence of second-generation, or new, peacekeeping, best defined as U.N. operations, authorized by the political organs or the Secretary-General, responsible for overseeing or executing the political solution of an inter-state or internal conflict, with the consent of the parties. It shares with the first generation the fundamental prerequisite of the consent of the parties, but seeks to implement peace, not to freeze conflicts in place. These missions have the following salient features:

- They are not limited to an exclusively military mandate, but can have a substantial or predominantly non-military mandate and composition involving electoral oversight; supervision of civil administration; promotion of human rights; supervision of law and order; economic rehabilitation; repatriation of refugees; humanitarian relief; de-mining assistance; public information; and training of governmental officials.

- Because the implementation of a settlement is likely to involve ongoing disputes between the parties, the new peacekeeping includes *peacemaking*, as the United Nations serves as a continuous mediator to help the parties bridge their differences.

- The new peacekeeping includes the broad notion of *peace building*—creating the conditions for the long-term preservation of the peace brought about by the settlement. The United Nations promotes reconciliation between or among the former combatants and assists them in responding to long-term national needs.

■ The operations are as likely to respond to a so-called internal conflict as to an inter-state conflict. Indeed, purely internal conflicts are practically a mythological beast.

■ The missions include numerous types of actors. While first-generation operations engaged primarily states and military personnel under U.N. auspices, the new peacekeeping includes guerrilla movements, indigenous political parties, regional organizations, non-governmental organizations, the specialized and technical agencies of the United Nations, and international financial institutions.

■ The new peacekeeping is a fluid phenomenon. The United Nations may adjust the mandate of an operation to respond to the political situation on the ground, adding or eliminating tasks at the behest of the parties and the international community. Personnel deployed before a settlement is reached may later receive a new mandate to help implement the settlement.

**Peace enforcement** lacks the essential prerequisite for peacekeeping—the consent of the parties to the operation, before or after a final settlement. Instead, peace enforcement represents the deployment by the U.N.'s political organs of military personnel to engage in non-consensual action, which may include the use of force, to restore international peace and security. Until the Gulf War, the only peace-enforcement activity had been the U.N. action in Korea, although some have suggested that parts of the 1960–64 Congo mission amounted to peace enforcement. Since 1990, the United Nations has engaged in peace enforcement in two ways: 1) by authorizing member states to take forcible actions—as with the Gulf War, the original U.S. intervention in Somalia in December 1992, and the U.S. intervention in Haiti in September 1994; or 2) by authorizing an existing U.N. peacekeeping mission to take action regardless of the will of the immediate parties—as the United Nations did in giving enforcement powers to the U.N. Operation in Somalia (UNOSOM) and the U.N. Protection Force (UNPROFOR) in early 1993.

# BASIC LEGAL AND POLITICAL FOUNDATIONS FOR U.N. INVOLVEMENT

## LEGAL COMPETENCE OF THE ORGANIZATION

The legal underpinnings of U.N. activity in the area of peacemaking, peacekeeping, and peace enforcement lie in the Charter of the United Nations, but they have been substantially augmented by the practices of the U.N.'s organs since 1945.

As a most basic matter, the Charter of the United Nations mentions neither the terms peacemaking, peacekeeping, peace enforcement, nor peace building. But the United Nations and its members have never interpreted the Charter so narrowly, searching for a specific authorization for each new activity. Rather, seeing it as a dynamic, *constitutive* instrument, they have asked whether a proposed U.N. activity is consistent with the principles and purposes of the United Nations and is nowhere precluded, an approach endorsed by the International Court of Justice early in the U.N.'s history in the *Reparation* case.[1] By this measure, the United Nations has demonstrable competence for all of the above functions.

Article 1 lists the first purpose of the Organization as "maintain[ing] international peace and security," including through "bring[ing] about by peaceful means . . . adjustment or settlement of international disputes or situations which might lead to a breach of the peace." This core U.N. function mirrors an obligation upon all states in Article 2 to "settle their international disputes by peaceful means in such a manner that international peace and security, and justice, are not endangered." Chapter VI of the Charter (Pacific Settlement of Disputes) elaborates the U.N.'s role in the peaceful, consensual settlement of disputes, in requiring parties to a dispute to seek a solution through one of a number of peaceful means and continuing with provisions for involvement of the various U.N. organs. Chapter VII (Action with Respect to Threats to the Peace, Breaches of the Peace, and Acts of Aggression) describes the process by which the United Nations is to respond to threats to and breaches of the peace, including through enforcement of Security Council decisions by sanctions and military force.

Other provisions in the Charter grant the Organization additional competence in these matters. Article 1 says the United Nations should "achieve international co-operation in solving international problems of an economic, social, cultural, or humanitarian character, and in promoting and encouraging respect for human rights and for fundamental freedoms for all. . . ." Article 55 expands upon this, requiring the United Nations to promote higher standards of living, solutions to social and economic problems, and "universal respect for . . . human rights and fundamental freedoms. . . ."

States opposing U.N. involvement in their conflicts have tended to assert one Charter-based defense to block U.N. action—Article 2, paragraph 7 of the Charter, which prohibits the Organization from "interven[ing] in matters which are essentially within the domestic jurisdiction of any state," except when the Security Council is applying enforcement measures. This argument can be quickly dismissed, however.

As an initial matter, Article 2(7) explicitly does *not* cover peace enforcement activities. Second, the trends of decision in international law have sharply curtailed, if not eliminated, the scope of Article 2(7) as a legal bar to peacemaking and peacekeeping. As was first recognized by the International Court of Justice, the concept of matters "essentially within the domestic jurisdiction of any state" has changed over time and "depends upon the development of international relations."[2] It clearly no longer covers attempts by the Organization to improve human rights situations in countries or to end their civil conflict. The minimal acquiescence to and sometime active support of the missions in Namibia, Haiti, Nicaragua, Angola, El Salvador, Cambodia, Somalia, and Mozambique also suggest that the international community sees the United Nations as competent to handle these matters.

Third, Article 2(7) prohibits the Organization from "interven[-ing]" in domestic affairs. Whatever the precise meaning of the term "intervention," peacemaking, peacekeeping, and peace building by definition flow from the consent of all the parties to the conflict (including all the relevant factions in an internal conflict), precluding its characterization as "intervention" in the internal affairs of a state.

## POLITICAL WILL

If the claims based on invocations of non-interference ultimately fail as arguments precluding consent-based operations, the U.N.'s ability to mount these missions faces its most pertinent challenge from the member states that comprise it. For all operations, consent-based and non-consensual, require the support of key member states—including the permanent members, large financial contributors, and important developing world nations. Acting formally through the vote of a political organ or through more informal methods, these key member states must concur upon the necessity of the mission. The international community must have an active interest in supporting directly, and in a sustained way, the peace process in the affected state or states. This support must be evinced in three ways: diplomatically, financially, and through donations of personnel.

The backing of those member states contributing personnel to peacekeeping and peace-enforcement operations—all the military forces, as well as numerous civilians seconded from government and the private sector—is particularly crucial. Donors will be motivated by their national interest in the operation—pursuing agendas from regional stability to the promotion of democracy. A broad array of states now participate, including both the permanent members and the affected state's immediate neighbors; these states were previously excluded from missions, but their participation is now often considered evidence of important political support.

Supervening the donors' foreign policy motivations for conferring their personnel, however, is another clear policy stance—avoidance of harm to their nationals. While many recent operations present few dangers to personnel—the election missions in Haiti, Nicaragua, and Eritrea, and the Namibia operation, for instance—violence has erupted in others, such as Cambodia, Somalia, and Yugoslavia. When threats occur against mission personnel, donors can be counted on to pressure the United Nations to modify the mandate, or to redeploy, protect, or withdraw the endangered staff. The participation of staff from the permanent members adds to that pressure, especially if they have donated many troops and civilians. If unsatisfied, donors may withdraw their military contingents (civilians being free to depart in any case).

The Secretary-General must thus negotiate not only with the immediate parties, but with these donors, to maintain their support. He can face a complete schism between the mandate of the Council to proceed with the mission and the hesitancy of donors—including those very Council members that approved the mandate—to donate personnel or place them in harm's way. For peace-enforcement missions, these issues are especially vexing.[3] With UNOSOM and UNPROFOR, key donor states—the United States, the United Kingdom, and France—seeking to avoid casualties, have refrained from approving expansive and proactive mandates for U.N. forces.

# LEGAL AND INSTITUTIONAL COMPETENCE OF U.N. ORGANS

## THE SECURITY COUNCIL

The Security Council has taken a leading role in all forms of U.N. peace efforts, especially through its creation of nearly all peace-keeping and peace-enforcement missions. As the organ endowed by the Charter with "the primary responsibility for the maintenance of international peace and security,"[4] the Security Council has a constitutionally mandated special competence in this area. With regard to *peacemaking*, Chapter VI of the Charter empowers the Council to make recommendations to the parties regarding the settlement of the dispute. These recommendations may provide guidelines for a final settlement, as has occurred in U.N. resolutions on the Middle East, the Iran-Iraq War, and elsewhere.

As for *peacekeeping*, legal scholars have searched for a textual basis in the Charter allowing the Council to dispatch first-generation missions to supervise truces. Attention has focused upon Article 36, found in Chapter VI, which allows the Council to "recommend appropriate procedures or methods of adjustment" of any dispute referred to it; and Article 40, in Chapter VII, which allows the Council, in the event of a threat to or breach of the peace, to "call upon the parties concerned to comply with such provisional measures as it deems necessary or desirable . . . without prejudice to the rights, claims, or position of the parties concerned." Yet both diplomats and legal scholars recognize that neither Charter section quite captures the essence of peacekeeping. Former Secretary-General Dag Hammarskjöld summed up the limits of textual exegesis in his quip that the Security Council created peacekeeping missions under Chapter "VI½."

The first thirty years of peacekeeping led to an abandonment of a search for particular Charter provisions to justify peacekeeping. Instead, the international community came to recognize the constitutive nature of the Charter, and it accepted the necessity for the Council to have broad discretion to act in furtherance of the principles and purposes of the Organization, as long as the Charter does not explicitly preclude such action. This doctrine of implied powers suggests an expansive scope of authority for the organs: That which is not prohibited is permitted. This ended most debate over the Council's competence to create early peacekeeping missions.

For second-generation operations, a search for a specific Charter reference for the Council's resolutions has proved equally frustrating. Instead, as with earlier missions, the Council has acted under a broad construction of Chapters VI, "VI½," and VII, as well as Article 24, which, as noted, grants the United Nations "primary responsibility" for the maintenance of international peace. A consensus has emerged that these parts of the Charter remain most pertinent, without an attempt to identify individual authorizing articles.

Finally, though peacekeeping can be based upon either Chapter VI or Chapter VII of the Charter, *peace enforcement* can be based only upon Chapter VII, which alone gives the Council the authority to enforce its decisions. Thus the distinction between Chapter VI and Chapter VII is not the same as that between peacekeeping and peace enforcement. A self-styled Chapter VI mission can only be peacekeeping, while a Chapter VII mission can include peacekeeping, peace enforcement, or both. For example, during the Yugoslavia mission, the Council explicitly invoked Chapter VII in reauthorizing UNPROFOR's duties in Croatia and Bosnia-Herzegovina in 1993. The invocation did not *per se* turn all of UNPROFOR's duties in those two territories into non-consensual peace enforcement. Indeed, much of its work remained based solely on consent. But it did give UNPROFOR legal power to undertake some of its duties—such as protection of "safe areas"—with or without the parties' consent. The mission thus includes enforcement as well as consent-based peacekeeping.

## THE GENERAL ASSEMBLY

The Assembly has been relegated to a smaller role in U.N. peacemaking and peacekeeping. While its resolutions may play an important part in signaling to the parties the will of the international community on their conflict, the organ is too large to supervise many operational tasks. It did create the mission in Sinai and West New Guinea (West Irian), the Haiti election (1990) and civilian (1993) missions, and the Eritrean election mission. Article 10 gives the Assembly the authority to discuss *any* matter within the scope of the Charter and to make recommendations to the member states and the Security Council, unless the Council is engaged in enforcement action on the same matter. Articles 11(2) and 14 specify that these may include recommendations related, respectively, to "the maintenance of international peace and security" as well as any other situation "which it deems likely to impair the general welfare or friendly relations among nations." Article 13 extends this power to recommendations on economic, social, cultural, educational, health, and human rights matters. These grants of authority, viewed in conjunction with the implied powers of all the organs, have been regarded by the U.N.'s members as providing the Assembly sufficient legal competence to engage in certain peace efforts.

The Assembly's greatest authority remains, however, its power under Article 17 of the Charter to approve the budget of the United Nations. The Assembly's budgetary power constitutes a critical source of influence and a check on the Security Council and the secretariat. Although the Assembly is unlikely to make fundamental changes to the budget proposed by the Secretary-General, it will, working closely with planners in the secretariat and the Security Council, scrutinize and adjust the plan. Moreover, the Assembly may move toward a more active role in peace efforts if many developing states continue to regard the Security Council as controlled by the larger states, and ongoing efforts to alter the Council's membership do not address these concerns sufficiently. The Assembly and the Council could also agree that the Assembly would assume more oversight over the non-military aspects of second-generation operations.

## THE SECRETARY-GENERAL

The heaviest mantle of responsibility within the U.N. system for peacemaking, peacekeeping, and peace enforcement falls upon the Secretary-General. Yet the Charter also offers the most meager direction for the person and office with the greatest responsibilities. Four articles suggest constitutional starting points for his duties. Article 97 empowers him as the "chief administrative officer of the Organization." Article 98 instructs him to "perform such other functions as are entrusted to him by [the political] organs." Article 99 permits him to bring to the Security Council's attention "any matter which in his opinion may threaten the maintenance of international peace and security." And Article 101 permits him to pick the secretariat's staff at his discretion with prime consideration for their competence and "due regard" for geographic diversity.

A search for constitutional underpinnings quickly yields results similar to those of earlier quests for the Charter basis for Council action. As Paul Szasz, who has been for many years a senior U.N. legal officer, has stated, "The fact is that the Secretary-General can in the political field do what he can get away with, i.e., in a given situation what the competent representative organs will encourage or at least tolerate. . . . "[5] This frank recognition of the implied powers of the office corresponds to a long trend of decisions by member states regarding the lawful authority of the Secretary-General. What he can "get away with" has been the product of nearly fifty years of U.N. history that reveal a constant accretion of authority by the Secretary-General in promoting the peaceful settlement of disputes. Indeed, the Secretary-General's legal footing in this regard is now so well established that member states rarely discuss it, and he no longer invokes a specific Charter basis for his action.

Beneath the Secretary-General work hundreds, even thousands, of people on peace efforts. At the apex are the *Under-Secretaries-General* for Political Affairs and Peacekeeping Affairs. Each particular effort is typically headed by a *Special Representative of the Secretary-General (SRSG)*, who is a civilian political envoy. As the senior U.N. official in the territory, country, or region, the SRSG assumes control of the operation on a day-to-day basis, both its internal administrative aspects and its external political functions vis-à-vis the parties and the settlement process. He or she serves as the focal point within the U.N. system for that mission and is the central figure in it. To be most effective, this person should be politically acceptable to the parties; possess diplomatic, political, and managerial skills; have a generalist's outlook; possess some familiarity with the conflict; ideally have some international stature; and understand the workings of the United Nations. Beneath him or her works the U.N. civil service at headquarters, at the U.N. office in Geneva and other cities, and in the operation itself.

## NEUTRALITY AND IMPARTIALITY: OLD TENETS AND NEW DILEMMAS

In carrying out its peacemaking, peacekeeping, and peace-enforcement undertakings—sometimes simultaneously in one conflict—the Organization has begun to face new dilemmas. These stem from the traditional insistence of the United Nations, in the case of *peacekeeping*, and to a degree in *peacemaking*, to remain impartial regarding the underlying merits of the disputes between the parties. Thus, for example, the United Nations and observers typically speak of peacekeeping forces as "neutral," "disinterested," "impartial," or "unbiased." States have seen the United Nations as the best institution for peacekeeping not only based on its institutional expertise, but because they have viewed it as impartial compared with any alternative: The competing interests of states would be factored into any decisions of political organs, and the multinational nature of the bureaucracy—as required by Article 100 of the Charter[6]—would ensure their implementation in a balanced manner. This policy contrasts with the stance of regional organizations or *sui generis* peacekeeping forces, which are more vulnerable to pressure from powerful members and are not sufficiently distant from a conflict to be neutral as peacekeepers.

In the era of traditional peacekeeping, the United Nations sought impartiality and, due to the limited nature of its mandate, usually achieved it. It simply watched over a truce without taking sides. As for peacemaking, the Secretary-General would often serve as an impartial mediator between the parties. His position would prove more delicate if the political organs had opined on the merits of the dispute. Although he might try to distance himself from the position of the political organs, he could not act in contravention of their mandate, and one party could remain suspicious of him (thus preventing any effective role in, for example, the Middle East peace process).

The U.N.'s increasingly assertive role in settling conflicts has further complicated the question of impartiality. The Security Council has take firm positions on a number of conflicts that increase the sense of mistrust of the U.N. as peacemaker. More important, second-generation peacekeeping has intruded the United Nations into the implementation of political settlements in a way that inevitably affects the relative power of the belligerents. It also changes the policy through the effects of peace building.

Impartiality can thus be threatened in a number of ways: First, when parties refuse to cooperate with U.N. peacemaking and peacekeeping efforts, the United Nations may need to take a position against the uncooperative party. Such responses could occur through actions of the peacekeepers in the country or its political organs. Such actions might include resolutions or sanctions to pressure the recalcitrant party. The U.N.'s reactions do not *per se* compromise the principle of impartiality—since the United

Nations is only taking a stance vis-à-vis one party in response to a specific action, rather than any predisposition. As Hammarskjöld stated in his 1961 Oxford speech, "[T]he international civil servant cannot be accused of lack of neutrality simply for taking a stand on a controversial issue when that is his duty and cannot be avoided."[7] But the violating party may well perceive the Organization as partial. A perception of favoritism can undermine the U.N.'s role as mediator and administrator of settlements. The United Nations thus faces a core dilemma: If it relies heavily upon mediation to resolve disputes, the parties may regard it as weak; if it attempts to push forward a peace plan through more assertive means, the recalcitrant party may regard it as biased.

This quandary becomes even more severe if an operation combines mandates of peacekeeping, with its requirement of impartiality, and *peace enforcement*, which lacks any such stricture, as occurred in the Somalia and Yugoslavia missions in 1993 and 1994. The U.N.'s responses to violations of Security Council resolutions through peace enforcement and the eventual use of force caused the uncooperative parties—the clan of Mohammed Farah Aidid and the Bosnian Serb forces, respectively—to label the United Nations as a party to the dispute rather than an impartial peacekeeper. The combination of conceptually different tasks required the United Nations to predict whether such force would undermine its credibility as a fair mediator or, conversely, would push the recalcitrant side to return to the bargaining table. The on-again, off-again nature of the peace talks in both Somalia and the former Yugoslavia belied any simple causal relationships.

Second, the U.N.'s self-interest may cause it to favor one party over another. If the Organization senses that one side acts more constructively or politely, or somehow can advance other U.N. agendas in the long run, it may, in subtle ways, prove more sympathetic to its positions than to those of the other side. Incumbent governments, with pre-existing ties to U.N. officials and a greater ability than opposition groups to influence events, may be the recipients of favorable treatment.

Third, the interests of individual states can become intertwined in new peacekeeping and peace-enforcement operations. Interested states can seek to influence a mission by pressuring the Secretary-General, by seconding personnel sympathetic to national concerns, or even by exercising control over officials seconded to missions in violation of Article 100 of the Charter. The issue is of greater import today as nationals of powerful states routinely hold senior positions. National biases also pose a more significant threat today because of the large civilian presence in peacekeeping operations. These personnel do not operate in a military chain of command under a U.N. force commander; moreover, their political duties leave room for more discretion and susceptibility to outside influence than military personnel would ordinarily have.

## GAUGING THE "SUCCESS" OF A U.N. MISSION

Instead of attempting any comprehensive review of U.N. peace-making, peacekeeping, and peace enforcement, it seems better to serve a cautionary notice regarding the desire of policy-makers to determine the success of a mission. In fact, success can be viewed from a number of perspectives: Is a mission successful only if it accomplishes its entire mandate as defined by the Security Council? Is it successful if it removes an item from the agenda of the international community? This determination must take into account those factors beyond the control of the United Nations, in order to avoid the suggestion that a "failure" is the sole fault of the United Nations or a "success" totally of its making. Unless one is willing to assume that the Organization, if only it had enough troops, money, and other resources, could end any armed conflict—hardly a realistic set of assumptions—one must approach things somewhat relatively and focus upon the effect of a U.N. mission upon the situation in the particular country or countries. From this perspective, one might hazard an assessment that, among recently established missions, those in Namibia, Cambodia, Nicaragua, Eritrea, South Africa, and El Salvador represent qualified successes. Those in Haiti and Angola can be labeled failures. The conflicts in Somalia, Western Sahara, Mozambique, Liberia, and the former Yugoslavia are still in too much a state of flux to allow even a preliminary judgment.

## A FINAL WORD

This short paper has attempted to review the conceptual and legal underpinnings of a new generation of U.N. activities in the field of international peace and security. Much needs to be discussed regarding measures to improve the institutional capacity of the Organization to perform its activities effectively, such as reform of the secretariat and the appropriate level of oversight of operations by New York–based actors. If peacemaking, peacekeeping, and peace-enforcement missions continue to proliferate, the U.N.'s members must immediately devote sustained political, financial, and personnel resources to them.

## NOTES

[1]See "Reparation for Injuries Suffered in the Service of the United Nations," 1949 ICJ 174, 182–83 (Apr. 11); reaffirmed in "Certain Expenses of the United Nations" (Article 17, paragraph 2, of the Charter), 1962 ICJ 151, 167–68 (July 20).

[2]Advisory Opinion No. 4, "Nationality Decrees Issued in Tunis and Morocco," 1923 PCIJ (Ser. B) No. 4, at 23 (Feb. 7).

[3]One UNPROFOR general states, "I don't read the Security Council resolutions any more because they don't help me" and finds a "fantastic gap" between resolutions and political will. "U.N. Bosnia Commander Wants More Troops, Fewer Resolutions," *The New York Times*, Dec. 31, 1993, p. A3.

[4]U.N. Charter, Art. 24(1).

[5]Paul C. Szasz, "The Role of the U.N. Secretary-General: Some Legal Aspects," 24 *New York University Journal of International Law and Politics* 161, 191 (1991).

[6]Article 100 states in pertinent part:

> In the performance of their duties the Secretary-General and the staff shall not seek or receive instructions from any government or from any other authority external to the organization. . . . Each Member of the United Nations undertakes to respect the exclusively international character of the responsibilities of the Secretary-General and the staff and not to seek to influence them in the discharge of their responsibilities.

[7]"The International Civil Servant in Law and Fact," in *Servant of Peace* (Wilder Foote, ed., 1962), p. 348.

| MASAHIKO ASADA | PEACEMAKING, PEACEKEEPING, AND PEACE ENFORCEMENT: CONCEPTUAL AND LEGAL UNDERPINNINGS OF THE U.N. ROLE |
|---|---|

The end of the Cold War has breathed new life into the United Nations. The Security Council is now virtually freed from the veto system[1] and, at the same time, its security functions are much more needed than at any other period since the United Nations was established. As the Gulf War demonstrated, the United Nations, its member states, and the peoples of the world assumed that the United Nations could now play the pivotal role in the maintenance of international peace and security that had been assigned to it by its founders.

Such expectations of the "new" United Nations led to the first-ever summit meeting of the Security Council in New York City on January 31, 1992. In the declaration of the meeting, the leaders present unanimously requested that Secretary-General Boutros Boutros-Ghali submit his "analysis and recommendations on ways of strengthening and making more efficient . . . the capacity of the United Nations for preventive diplomacy, peacemaking and peacekeeping."[2] In response, the Secretary-General provided in his report of June 1992, entitled *An Agenda for Peace,*[3] a series of recommendations, including such fresh or refreshed ideas as preventive deployment of U.N. forces, establishment of peace-enforcement units, and post-conflict peace building.

Two years since, things do not seem to be going precisely as he expected the organization to proceed. The picture of U.N. peace operations during the interim is at best a mixed blessing and falls between success and failure in terms of the accomplishment of the mandated tasks. While succeeding in Namibia (an operation before *An Agenda for Peace*), Cambodia, and so far in the former Yugoslav Republic of Macedonia, the United Nations has suffered considerable blows to its credibility as the world peace organization in Bosnia-Herzegovina and Somalia, to take the most serious and eye-catching cases, as well as in Angola, Haiti, Rwanda, and elsewhere to a somewhat lesser extent. The Secretary-General himself in his recent report admitted that "the optimism which prevailed one year ago has been diminished as a result of the difficulties encountered in the field, especially in Somalia and former Yugoslavia."[4]

What are the causes of the failures? This chapter will first draw a picture of the U.N. security system based on the Charter of the United Nations as well as its subsequent practices. It will next try to identify the fresh elements and new trends in post–Cold War U.N. peace activities and for each category of the new-wave activities will evaluate its merits and demerits in light of the problems it is now encountering as well as other problems it may potentially confront. This approach should help to reveal some of the causes of recent U.N. failures. Finally, some recommendations will be explored to reverse any negative tendencies and to refashion the new-wave activities, so that the United Nations may better function in the field of international peace and security. In this study, the main focus will be placed on U.N. peacekeeping operations, as they are the most salient among the rapidly growing U.N. peace activities,[5] though other peace-related measures may also be referred to, as appropriate.

## THE CONCEPTUAL FOUNDATIONS OF TRADITIONAL U.N. APPROACHES TO PEACE

Traditionally, there are essentially three approaches to the maintenance of international peace and security in the U.N. framework: peacemaking, peacekeeping, and peace enforcement. *Peacemaking*,[6] according to the definition by the Secretary-General, means "action to bring hostile parties to agreement, essentially through such peaceful means as those foreseen in Chapter VI of the Charter of the United Nations." In other words, pacific settlement of disputes. Similarly, *peace enforcement* can be defined as action to maintain or restore international peace and security through such coercive military or non-military enforcement measures as those provided for in Chapter VII of the Charter, which constitutes the core of the U.N. collective security system.[7]

Unlike these two original functions of the United Nations, *peacekeeping*—a peace effort through military (and civilian) presence under U.N. command interposed between hostile states or hostile communities within a state—was not envisaged in the U.N. Charter, but was born out of U.N. practice. While opinions on its constitutional basis are, therefore, varied, the United Nations seems to satisfy itself by putting in a new "Chapter VI$\frac{1}{2}$." It explains that peacekeeping operations fall short of the provisions of Chapter VII (peace enforcement) and go beyond purely diplomatic means or those described in Chapter VI (peacemaking).[8] In any event, no one denies that peacekeeping operations have been accepted as constitutional by U.N. member states as a whole. Rather, they arguably became "the" peace functions of the United Nations during the Cold War era in the near absence of effective collective security measures.

Although peacekeeping has not been, and still is not, based on any particular doctrine, its long-cumulative practices have developed a series of guiding principles for such operations.[9] They include four basic rules: non-interference in the internal affairs of the host state; the exclusion of interested countries from participation; the consent of the host state; and the use of force only in self-defense. Simply put, the first two rules are meant to assure the impartiality of peacekeepers, while the latter two make the operations non-enforcing, though these two groups are more interrelated than independent.

The impartial and non-enforcing character of peacekeeping activities aptly represents their limited aims. As *An Agenda for Peace* describes, peacekeeping is a technique that expands the "possibilities" for both the prevention of conflict and the making of peace.[10] It is aimed at a mere temporary, provisional solution to a conflict and not its final settlement.[11] Therefore, it would be pointless to criticize peacekeeping operations as incapable of solving the conflicts themselves.

The meaning of "peace" in *peacekeeping* is accordingly limited in scope. "Peace" to be kept by U.N. peacekeeping operations[12] signifies something different from its usual meaning—that is, the non-existence of war or armed conflict. Instead it covers only a period of temporary cessation of hostilities during an armed conflict. Such provisional "peace" is the basis on which peacekeeping operations primarily recur. If, therefore, such provisional "peace" is broken and hostilities recur, the peacekeepers would lose the basis for their activities.

All these characteristics of peacekeeping are in impressive contrast with those of the two other U.N. approaches to peace, namely, peacemaking and peace enforcement. *Peacemaking,* as is evident from the fact that it is a metaphorical expression for the peaceful settlement of disputes, refers to and is designed for the final settlement of disputes. Assuming that a dispute develops from a difference of opinions and escalates to an armed conflict, passes through a ceasefire agreement, and is brought to its final settlement, peacemaking covers virtually the whole spectrum of a dispute and its ultimate purpose is to put an end to it. In that sense, "peace" in peacemaking is much broader in scope than is "peace" in peacekeeping, and it is even broader still than its usual meaning of non-existence of an armed conflict.

The other peace approach, *peace enforcement*, does not deal with the whole process of dispute settlement, but covers only part of it as in the case of peacekeeping. It does not, however, address the same part of a dispute as does peacekeeping: Peace enforcement pays more attention to the military aspects of a conflict. Article 39 of the U.N. Charter, which is the pivotal provision of its Chapter VII, lists three specific situations where the Security Council may take enforcement measures to maintain or restore international peace and security: threat to the peace, breach of the peace, and act of aggression. Hence, "peace" in peace enforcement signifies the non-existence of these situations.

What these three specific situations mean in reality is an open question. The U.N. Charter does not give any definitions of them and leaves much discretion to the Security Council about whether to resort to enforcement measures. In forty-nine years of U.N. history, there is not a single case in which the Council determined the existence of an act of aggression. On the other hand, more frequent determinations have been made as to the existence of a "threat to the peace." The existence of a "threat to the peace" tends to be determined mainly in intra-state (civil) conflicts, while that of a "breach of the peace" occurs exclusively in inter-state confrontations. The scope of the former concept has been made so large as to cover even situations where it is not easy to find the relevance to *international peace and security*. In addition to the classic cases of the apartheid policy of South Africa and the unilateral declaration of independence by South Rhodesia, we have recently seen an increasing number of cases where the concept of a "threat to the peace" is impressively broadened.[13] The concept of "peace" in peace enforcement has accordingly been enlarged.

Thus each of the three peace-related activities of the United Nations—peacemaking, peacekeeping, and peace enforcement—has its own *raison d'être*. Nevertheless, these three approaches to peace do not seem to cover everything that is related to a dispute or a conflict. Among those areas where the traditional U.N. peace mechanism is lacking or insufficient are the prevention of a dispute or a conflict, post-conflict tensions, and situations where hostilities recur after a ceasefire agreement has been reached and peacekeepers deployed. Although some of the approaches he proposed had already been pursued to a limited extent previously, in *An Agenda for Peace*, Secretary-General Boutros-Ghali tried to fill or at least to narrow these gaps by emphasizing preventive diplomacy and preventive deployment of peacekeepers, post-conflict peace building, and the establishment of peace enforcement units.

"Preventive diplomacy,"[14] according to *An Agenda for Peace*, means action to prevent disputes from arising between parties, to prevent existing disputes from escalating into conflicts, and to limit the spread of the latter when they occur. With this broad definition, preventive diplomacy covers part of an area that is also for peacekeeping. But its centerpiece appears to lie in preventing disputes from arising or escalating into conflicts. Preventive diplomacy would therefore function best early in "peacetime" when disputes are still latent.

At the other end of the spectrum of U.N. peace efforts is the concept of "peace building," which, according to *An Agenda for Peace*, is defined as action to identify and support structures that will tend to strengthen and solidify peace in order to avoid a relapse into conflict. "Peace" in this case signifies something more perpetual than, and to be sought subsequent to, the peace attained through peacemaking.

Hence, preventive diplomacy and peace building, as introduced by Secretary-General Boutros-Ghali, perhaps go beyond what is envisaged by traditional peacemaking or peacekeeping, let alone peace enforcement. Or, it may be said that their introduction helps re-emphasize the importance of what has been more or less overlooked thus far in U.N. peacemaking or peacekeeping efforts, if one adopts a broader sense of the terms.

## PEACEKEEPING COMBINED WITH PREVENTIVE DIPLOMACY OR PEACE BUILDING

U.N. peacekeeping operations have increased considerably in number and size over the last few years. In the span of only six years (1988–93), far more operations than in the previous forty years (1948–87) have been launched.[15] They include the first such operations in continental Europe (former Yugoslavia) and in the former Soviet Union (Georgia).

The size of any one given operation has also been expanded. During the "first generation" or "traditional" peacekeeping period (until 1987),[16] the maximum strength of a given operation was something between hundreds and several thousands, with the exception of the U.N. Force in the Congo (ONUC), where some 20,000 personnel were deployed. The "second generation" or "new wave" peacekeeping (from 1988 to the present),[17] however, includes such large-scale operations as the U.N. Transitional Authority in Cambodia (UNTAC), the U.N. Protection Force (UNPROFOR, in the former Yugoslavia), and the U.N. Operation in Somalia II (UNOSOM-II), which has personnel strength between 20,000 and 40,000. In mid-1993, more than 80,000 U.N. personnel were deployed in the field.

All that said, one of the most outstanding features of "second generation" peacekeeping lies in the fact that the tasks and missions are dramatically broadened to include those which are beyond the scope of the traditional peacekeeping concept.

## PEACEKEEPING WITH PEACE-BUILDING FUNCTIONS

In traditional peacekeeping, the main tasks were to supervise the ceasefire and to prevent the recurrence of hostilities. In that sense, traditional peacekeeping functions were essentially passive and were meant only to defend the status quo by interposing a buffer between hostile parties: Their immediate aim was to give the peacemakers both the time and the environment to negotiate a settlement of the dispute. Yet, there was no guarantee that the peacemakers would succeed. The criticism that has been made of some peacekeeping operations, such as the U.N. Peacekeeping Force in Cyprus (established in 1964) and the U.N. Interim Force in Lebanon (established in 1978), is that they merely extend their mandate for decades without having any prospects for solving the underlying problems.[18] However, some of the post–Cold War U.N. operations have combined peacekeeping with other peace-related functions and have integrated the final settlement of the dispute into one comprehensive peace program. Indeed, this has been the area of most rapid growth in the new-generation peacekeeping efforts.

The first such operation was the U.N. Transition Assistance Group (UNTAG), which was set up in April 1989 to supervise the implementation of the U.N. plan for Namibia's transition to independence. In this operation, the U.N. peacekeepers did carry out such traditional peacekeeping tasks as monitoring the ceasefire and the reduction and eventual removal of the South African military presence in Namibia. But these functions served only as conditions for accomplishing the central objective of the operation: namely, "to ensure the early independence of Namibia through free elections under the supervision and control of the United Nations."

Fulfilling this mandate required UNTAG to be equipped with a wide variety of functions, which were mostly beyond those of traditional peacekeeping. These functions included preparation and supervision of the electoral processes, reception and resettlement of Namibian exiles in time to vote, and monitoring of the local police to ensure that they fulfilled their duty of maintaining law and order in an efficient and non-partisan manner. Such a complicated mission necessitated a structural change of the operation, with the civilian personnel, including police, playing a sizable role.

However, the most important earmark of this type of peacekeeping operation is that, unlike traditional ones, it is established or dispatched after the negotiations for a final settlement of disputes have been completed. In the case of UNTAG, a tripartite agreement allowing implementation of Security Council Resolution 435 (1978), which had virtually approved a plan for a comprehensive settlement of the Namibian conflict and had established UNTAG,[19] was agreed upon and signed on December 22, 1988, before the peacekeepers were actually sent to the field in April 1989.

Another operation of the same type was UNTAC, which was established by Resolution 745 in February 1992 to supervise various parts of the existing administration, to organize elections, to monitor the police, to promote human rights, to repatriate refugees and begin rehabilitation of the country, and to carry out a familiar range of traditional military functions. In this case, too, a series of accords, including the "Agreement on a Comprehensive Political Settlement of the Cambodia Conflict," was signed beforehand on October 23, 1991, in Paris.[20]

Operations of this type have functioned not only as peacekeeping but also as peace-building or even nation-building operations, with the latter two much more emphasized. They have mainly addressed post-conflict situations in order to consolidate the peace attained through peacemaking efforts and to prevent the recurrence of violence. If traditional peacekeeping is described as activities in "Chapter VI½," the new operations just discussed might be labeled as operations in "Chapter VI¼," as they are approaching Chapter VI by encompassing more conflict resolution/prevention elements.

Such post-conflict activities are not, however, totally unprecedented in the history of U.N. peacekeeping. In the early 1960s, the U.N. Temporary Executive Authority (UNTEA) was established to buffer the transfer of administration from the Dutch to the Indonesian government in West New Guinea (West Irian). It was assisted by some 1,500 U.N. Security Force (UNSF) personnel in the task of maintaining law and order. The sending of these personnel was based on U.N. General Assembly Resolution 1752 (XVII), taking note of the Dutch-Indonesian agreement of August 15, 1962.[21] The agreement had provided a final settlement to the problem. Although, in terms of the organization, there apparently existed two separate U.N. operations in West Irian—UNTEA and UNSF—their overall combined function was comparable to UNTAG or UNTAC. In that sense, they were quite unique among traditional peacekeeping operations.

But now, such operations are no longer exceptions. Out of some twenty "post–Cold War" operations, one can count as examples falling into this category those in Angola, El Salvador, Mozambique, and, hopefully, Western Sahara, in addition to UNTAG and UNTAC. It seems that the end of the Cold War has made possible not only the final settlement of some of the conflicts, which had been more or less tied up in, and hung up with, the U.S.–Soviet rivalry, but also subsequent peace building for the prevention of conflict recurrence, and such post-conflict peace-building activities have been effectively combined with traditional peacekeeping operations.

## PREVENTIVE PEACEKEEPING

Operations covering the other end of the timeline of a conflict—the pre-conflict phase—should also be firmly placed in second-generation peacekeeping. Traditionally, peacekeeping operations have been mounted only after hostilities have already broken out and a ceasefire agreement has been reached. If, however, peacekeepers are delivered before a conflict has actually begun, that could prevent potential aggressors from launching an attack or could at least compel them to give a second thought to it. Contributions that such preventive U.N. deployment could make, it seems, have been contemplated most acutely since the experience of the Gulf crisis in 1990. If the United Nations had dispatched some symbolic U.N. troops beforehand to the Kuwaiti territory bordering Iraq, it might have prevented the latter's invasion of Kuwait.

Taking these considerations perhaps into account, the Secretary-General, in *An Agenda for Peace*, made the following recommendation regarding preventive peacekeeping:[22] "In inter-State disputes, when both parties agree, I recommend that if the Security Council concludes that the likelihood of hostilities between neighbouring countries could be removed by the preventive deployment of a United Nations presence on the territory of each State, such action should be taken. . . . In cases where one nation fears a cross-border attack, if the Security Council concludes that a United Nations presence on one side of the border, with the consent only of the requesting country, would serve to deter conflict, I recommend that preventive deployment take place."[23]

As the first application in the field of this recommendation, preventive peacekeepers in the "pre-conflict" phase have been dispatched, in accordance with Council Resolution 795 of December 11, 1992, to the territory of the former Yugoslav Republic of Macedonia upon its request, and so far they have been successful in preventing the conflict of the other part of the former Yugoslavia from spreading into that republic. Although the performance of preventive peacekeeping activities is not as conspicuous as other peacekeeping activities, nothing particular happening means success in this case.

Preventive peacekeeping appears to be a new invention of Secretary-General Boutros-Ghali, but, in reality, it is not. There is at least one case where peacekeepers were sent for preventive purposes: the U.N. Observation Group in Lebanon (UNOGIL), which was dispatched in June 1958 pursuant to Security Council Resolution 128, "to ensure that there is no illegal infiltration of personnel or supply of arms. . .across the Lebanese borders" from the Syrian part of the United Arab Republic. In this case, too, the U.N. presence successfully prevented the feared infiltration and supply from outside and thus the outbreak of a conflict.

## ASSESSMENT

The combination between peacekeeping on the one hand, and either peace building in the post-conflict phase or preventive diplomacy in the pre-conflict phase on the other, has now occupied a major part of U.N. peacekeeping operations. How can one assess such a phenomenon? Certainly, these two types of peacekeeping operations are quite different in functions, tasks, structure, size, nature of accompanying risks, and, of course, timing of delivery. Nevertheless, they seem to carry some essential characteristics in common, characteristics that are also shared by the traditional peacekeepers: a non-enforcing and pacific nature based on the consent and cooperation of the parties concerned and an impartial and neutral character. These common features seem to have some bearing on the fact that most of these enterprises have achieved a general success in accomplishing their mandated tasks.

Success so far is, however, no guarantee for the future. Regarding the *preventive deployment of peacekeepers*, concerns have been raised: If the request for a U.N. presence comes from only one (potential) party to a conflict, then the United Nations could become a party to the conflict by taking sides; and even if (potential) parties to a conflict agree on the preventive deployment, one of them may change its position and ask the United Nations to leave.[24] While the latter point is common to all peacekeeping activities based on consent and does no more than show their limit, the former problem, which has a more direct bearing on preventive peacekeeping, seems to go directly against the principle of impartiality to be maintained in the course of peacekeeping operations.

Sending peacekeepers based on the consent or request of only one (potential) party to a conflict is, however, not without precedent during the traditional peacekeeping era. For instance, although not a preventive-type deployment, the U.N. Emergency Force (UNEF) sent to the Middle East from 1956 to 1967 was based on the consent of only one party—Egypt—and therefore was deployed only on the Egyptian side of the Armistice Demarcation Line between Egypt and Israel. On the same basis, the United Nations made the decision to withdraw the UNEF in May 1967 when Egyptian consent was withdrawn.[25] A week after the U.N. troop withdrawal, Egypt closed the Tiran Strait, which was the first in a series of events that led eventually to the Six-Day War—which started with the Israeli preemptive strikes on Egypt, Syria, and Jordan.[26]

Before this development, Israel had already expressed its suspicion, in relation to the one-sided U.N. deployment, of a possible Egyptian military buildup behind the screen of the U.N. force.[27] The actuality was that the Israeli suspicion was not directed at the

U.N. presence only on the Egyptian side of the demarcation line, but toward the possibility of U.N. withdrawal through Egypt's unilateral decision.[28] Hence, one would have expected little complaint, if any, coming from Israel regarding U.N. impartiality. On the contrary, Israel wished to see the continued stationing of the U.N. force, independent of Egyptian consent. This seems to indicate that a one-sided deployment of U.N. peacekeepers should not necessarily be taken to be partial.

Nevertheless, the sheer fact remains that Israel did feel and express concerns about the overall system of the UNEF presence in the Middle East, which was dependent only on Egyptian consent, and that those concerns came true when the UNEF withdrew and the Tiran Strait was closed. Such concerns are quite reasonable, if only the party on whose side U.N. troops are stationed is bellicose. On the other hand, deploying peacekeepers only on the territory of the party that fears a cross-border attack could effectively deter such an attack, as *An Agenda for Peace* points out. If, for example, Israel had been thinking of attacking Egypt, the presence of UNEF in Egypt would have had a deterrent effect.

The problem is that, in the case of preventive deployment, it is usually quite difficult or almost impossible to know beforehand which of the potential parties to a conflict is likely to be the eventual aggressor, or to judge which of the parties concerned is the more bellicose. Thus preventive deployment of U.N. forces with only one-sided consent encompasses a double-edged danger: While it may serve to deter an act of aggression, it may also provide an eventual aggressor with a rare opportunity to prepare for an attack under the U.N. safeguard. Furthermore, if the United Nations adopts a case-by-case approach and tries to accord different treatments to the requests for a U.N. presence from different parties in accordance with its own judgment about their bellicosity, that would surely be criticized as introducing a double standard. As a result, the United Nations would have to send troops, if possible, to whichever party unilaterally requested its presence and would run the double-edged risk outlined above.

A second possible dilemma that preventive peacekeeping would involve is related to the timing of withdrawal. There is certainly no problem with U.N. withdrawal from an area if the risk of war there subsides. UNOGIL was deployed in Lebanon to ensure that no illegal infiltration of personnel or supply of arms from outside the country took place, and the group departed after a message from the Lebanese Foreign Minister made it known that the local situation had cooled.[29] However, a difficult problem regarding the withdrawal will reveal itself when the tensions run high and an armed attack appears forthcoming, and troop-contributing countries wish to withdraw as a consequence.

Obviously, if a potential aggressor actually commits an armed attack, the United Nations would have good reason to impose economic or military sanctions against it. In that sense, an actual withdrawal of the peacekeepers or even the appearance of a withdrawal in the face of a feared attack could possibly give the potential aggressor a warning that sanctions might come if it proceeds, and this might provide an effective deterrent against aggression.

Nevertheless, sanctions are not certain to come all the time, and hence the credibility of deterrence may attenuate. Moreover, a withdrawal of peacekeepers, apart from discrediting U.N. credibility, might give the would-be aggressor a wrong signal that the United Nations is retreating from the question. Such a withdrawal would surely make it easier for the determined aggressor to launch an attack, in the absence of the possibility of being blamed for attacking U.N. personnel. To counter such a miscalculation, it would be essential for the United Nations to be well equipped to take enforcement measures and to convey its intention of doing so.

Another new type of *peacekeeping operation*, which is *combined with peace building* and involves a comprehensive settlement of disputes, may also bear problems similar to those of preventive deployment, as far as U.N. impartiality is concerned. As the former Under-Secretary-General for Peacekeeping Operations, Marrack Goulding, points out, peacekeepers would face difficulties in remaining impartial if one of the parties failed to comply fully with its obligations under the agreed settlement.[30] This became a reality in Cambodia when UNTAC was confronted with the resistance of the Khmer Rouge, one of the four Cambodian factions, and was almost faced with an alternative of whether to carry out the mandate by force or to remain neutral. UNTAC was finally successful in accomplishing its mandate while keeping itself as neutral as possible among the factions.[31] It was eventually so, but such success is not always assured. What should be the course of action for the United Nations to take when it becomes apparent that attaining the mandate is impossible without using force? The question of the use of force by peacekeepers will be discussed later.

## PEACEKEEPING UNDER CHAPTER VII: THREE DIFFERENT CATEGORIES

The line of evolution discussed above is, though fresh in itself, still largely in conformity with the principles of traditional peacekeeping. Yet, "second generation" peacekeeping operations do contain those with mandates clearly beyond traditional peacekeeping principles. Such a drastic change can be seen especially in the fact that Chapter VII of the U.N. Charter is invoked in the resolution establishing a peacekeeping operation or broadening the mandate of one already set up. This is indeed revolutionary because, as was mentioned earlier, peacekeeping has been recognized as falling short of Chapter VII.

Peacekeepers with mandates under Chapter VII include 1) the U.N. Iraq-Kuwait Observation Mission (UNIKOM) (see Table 1), established by Security Council Resolution 689 (1991) as the first instance where Chapter VII was invoked in relation to this kind of

**Table 1. Resolutions and Events Related to UNIKOM and Iraq**

| Date | Res. | Ch. VII | Events |
|---|---|---|---|
| 8/6/90 | *661 | Y | SC decides to impose general economic sanctions against Iraq. |
| 11/29/90 | *678 | Y | SC authorizes member states to use all necessary means to restore peace in the area. |
| 4/3/91 | *687 | Y | SC sets terms for a formal ceasefire, including establishment of UNIKOM. |
| 4/6/91 | – | – | Iraq accepts Res. 687. (Formal ceasefire takes effect on 4/11/91.) |
| 4/9/91 | 689 | Y | SC establishes UNIKOM, to be terminated only by a SC decision. |
| 1/10/93 | – | – | Iraq illegally retrieves missiles and other weapons from Kuwait. |
| 2/5/93 | 806 | Y | SC authorizes UNIKOM to take physical action. (Weapons can be used only in self-defense.) |

*Note*: Resolutions with asterisk = enforcement measures independent of peacekeeping.

U.N. operation; 2) UNPROFOR[32] (see Table 2), which was deployed in accordance with Resolution 743 (1992), the mandate of which has been expanded to cover Chapter VII by Resolution 807 (1993) and some of the subsequent resolutions, including Resolution 836 (1993) in particular; and 3) UNOSOM-II (see Table 3), which was set up by Resolution 814 (1993) Part B, the mandate of which was later modified by Resolution 897 (1994). Thus listed, the implications of citing Chapter VII are not common in all cases, and there seem to be three different meanings in the same expression of Security Council resolutions, "acting under Chapter VII."

## OPERATIONS WITHOUT THE CONSENT OF THE HOST STATE

The first is related to the establishment of a peacekeeping operation and its continued presence in the field. Traditionally, one of the most important principles in establishing a peacekeeping operation is that it must be based on the consent of the host state, which derives from the principle of the territorial sovereignty of states. If, therefore, the host state withdraws its consent, peacekeepers have to leave, as in the case of UNEF in Egypt. However, when a U.N. operation is set up through Chapter VII, this principle does not automatically apply.

In the case of UNIKOM, the formal decision to dispatch the observer unit was taken by Security Council Resolution 689 of April 9, 1991, approving the Secretary-General's report on the implementation of part of Resolution 687 of April 3, 1991. The latter resolution had set conditions for a formal ceasefire between Iraq and the coalition forces, including the deployment of a U.N. observer unit (paragraph 5). Although, in formalistic terms, Iraq gave consent to the deployment of UNIKOM by accepting conditions for the ceasefire on April 6, it is, in substantive terms, questionable to say that this constituted a real consent. Rather, the establishment of UNIKOM seems to have been compulsory, with Iraqi consent coerced as part of the endgame package of the U.N. enforcement action against Iraq. Also, as regards UNIKOM's terms of mandate, Security Council Resolution 689 (1991) made clear that it could "only be terminated by a decision of the Council" (paragraph 2).

The mandate originally given to UNIKOM was impressively moderate despite the unique circumstances of its establishment—

**Table 2. Resolutions and Events Related to UNPROFOR and the Former Yugoslavia**

| Date | Res. | Ch. VII | Events |
|------|------|---------|--------|
| 9/25/91 | *713 | Y | SC decides to impose arms embargo against Yugoslavia. |
| 2/21/92 | 743 | | SC establishes UNPROFOR. |
| 5/30/92 | *757 | Y | SC decides to impose general economic sanctions against former republic of Yugoslavia. |
| 8/13/92 | *770 | Y | SC calls upon states to take all measures necessary to facilitate the delivery of humanitarian assistance in Bosnia. |
| 9/14/92 | 776 | | SC authorizes enlargement of UNPROFOR's mandate and strength in Bosnia. (UNPROFOR's full deployment in Bosnia.) |
| 12/11/92 | 795 | | SC authorizes preventive deployment of UNPROFOR in Macedonia. |
| 1/22/93 | – | – | Croatian army attacks areas under protection of UNPROFOR. |
| 2/19/93 | 807 | Y | SC invites SG to take all appropriate measures to strengthen the security of UNPROFOR. (Chap. VII is mentioned only to this end.) |
| 3/30/93 | 815 | Y | SC decides to extend UNPROFOR's mandate. (Chap. VII is mentioned only for security of UNPROFOR and its freedom of movement.) |
| 6/4/93 | 836 | Y | SC authorizes UNPROFOR to take the necessary measures (including use of force) in response to bombardments against the safe areas and member states to take all necessary measures, through the use of air power, in and around those areas to support UNPROFOR. |

*Note*: Resolutions with asterisk = enforcement measures independent of peacekeeping.

**45**

Table 3. Resolutions and Events Related to UNOSOM-II and Somalia

| Date | Res. | Ch. VII | Events |
|---|---|---|---|
| 1/23/92 | *733 | Y | SC decides to impose arms embargo against Somalia. |
| 4/24/92 | 751 | | SC establishes UNOSOM-I. |
| 12/3/92 | *794 | Y | SC authorizes SG and member states to use all necessary means to establish a secure environment for humanitarian relief operations in Somalia. |
| 3/26/93 | 814 | Y | SC establishes UNOSOM-II with enforcement powers. |
| 6/5/93 | – | – | Pakistani contingent of UNOSOM-II attacked. |
| 6/6/93 | 837 | Y | SC reaffirms that it is authorized under Res. 814 to take all necessary measures against those responsible for the attack. |
| 10/3/93 | – | – | U.S. Rangers launch operation to capture key aids of Gen. Aidid. |
| 10/4/93 | – | – | Humiliating treatment of the bodies of U.S. soldiers televised. |
| 10/10/93 | – | – | U.S. reportedly abandons efforts to capture Gen. Aidid. |
| 2/4/94 | 897 | Y | SC revises mandate for UNOSOM-II (without enforcement powers). |
| 11/4/94 | 954 | Y | SC decides to withdraw UNOSOM-II by the end of March 1995. |

*Note*: Resolutions with asterisk = enforcement measures independent of peacekeeping.

and although the military observers, for the first time in the history of U.N. peacekeeping, consisted of forces from all the permanent members of the Security Council and many of the U.N. members that participated in the coalition forces, which gave the appearance of a continuation of the enforcement action. UNIKOM's tasks were simply to monitor the Khor Abdullah waterway between Iraq and Kuwait and the demilitarized zone, to deter violations of the boundary through its presence, and to observe any hostile action from either side. The observers were therefore unarmed like other standard observer missions, until UNIKOM's terms of reference were extended later by Resolution 806 (1993).[33] UNIKOM was indeed playing "a traditional role in a most untraditional drama."[34]

Similarly, UNOSOM-II was established by Security Council Resolution 814 of March 26, 1993, without requiring the consent of the Somali "government," if one can use that term in this case. The Council resolution, precisely speaking, expanded the mandate of the original UNOSOM in accordance with the Secretary-General's report of March 3, 1993. As the report states, the deployment of UNOSOM-II "would not be subject to the agreement of any local faction leaders."[35] Although UNOSOM-II also has other characteristics arising from its establishment under Chapter VII (see below), it shares a common ground with UNIKOM on this particular point. Equally interesting is the fact that UNOSOM-II built on the efforts of the Gulf War–type coalition forces (Unified Task Force, or UNITAF) that were organized in accordance with Council Resolution 794 of December 3, 1992, to establish a secure environment for humanitarian relief operations in Somalia.

It seems, from the above examples,[36] that the establishment of a peacekeeping operation without the consent of the host state is only possible as part of, or in close relation to, simultaneous or preceding enforcement actions, even when its tasks are within the limits of traditional peacekeeping (as was the case with UNIKOM). Theoretically speaking, however, it is also possible to set up a peacekeeping operation without the consent of the state concerned, independently of related enforcement actions, if it is done under Chapter VII. Nevertheless, relying on Chapter VII in establishing an operation would not be appropriate, particularly if the mandated tasks are limited to those of traditional peacekeeping, because by doing so the neutral character of the operation would be taken away from the outset.

## OPERATIONS WITH ENHANCED SECURITY

The second purpose of resorting to Chapter VII is to show the U.N.'s firm and fixed determination by giving a clear message to those violating a previously agreed arrangement and attacking U.N. personnel that peacekeepers would use force, if necessary, in accordance with the authorization of the given mandate. The use of force in this case is, however, not beyond the limits of self-defense.

One of the examples of this kind of operation can be found in Security Council Resolution 807 of February 19, 1993, which referred to Chapter VII for the first time in the context of UNPROFOR operations. The resolution was adopted to extend the original mandate of UNPROFOR and to invite the Secretary-General to "take. . .all appropriate measures to strengthen the security of UNPROFOR [in Croatia], in particular by providing it with the necessary defensive means." (See paragraph 8.) This was an answer on the U.N. side to the Croatian offensive and the Serb reaction thereto in January 1993 in a number of locations of the U.N. Protected Areas,[37] which resulted in a loss of lives within UNPROFOR's French and other contingents.[38] Notwithstanding the fact that the Security Council determined the situation constituted "a threat to the peace and security in the region," it was acting under Chapter VII merely for the purpose of ensuring "the security of UNPROFOR," and for no more. In fact, the last preambular paragraph of the resolution where Chapter VII is referred to reads as follows: "Determined to ensure the security of UNPROFOR and *to this end*, acting under Chapter VII of the Charter of the United Nations, . . . " [emphasis added].

More importantly, the invocation of Chapter VII was interpreted by members of the Security Council to mean the strengthening of the "self-defence capability" of UNPROFOR and not to mean the authorization of the use of force beyond self-defense, nor its continued deployment without the necessary consent. In adopting the resolution, France, its original sponsor, underlined the idea by stating that its priority consideration was "the security of the forces" and the draft resolution was a response to the "overriding need to endow this Force with both the legal basis and the military means effectively to ensure its self-defence," and that it did not intend, by referring to Chapter VII, to "change the nature of the force" from a peacekeeping force.[39] China voted in favor of the draft resolution, "considering that the sponsor country has repeatedly stated that the purpose of invoking Chapter VII of the United Nations Charter is to take measures to increase appropriately UNPROFOR's self-defence capability."[40]

It should be concluded that the reference to Chapter VII in Resolution 807 (1993) was not meant to change the fundamental character of the peacekeepers. Instead, it simply expressed the U.N. determination to act in a firm manner against an attack on U.N. personnel and, to this end, to enhance the security of the personnel by providing them with the necessary defensive means. Although the reference to Chapter VII in the resolution was neither an abuse nor a misuse of the Chapter to the extent that it determined the existence of "a threat to peace and security within the region," the objective of the resolution seems to have been achieved without referring to Chapter VII.

Resolution 807 (1993) is not the only resolution of this kind. Another example can be found in Resolution 815, which was adopted on March 30, 1993, to follow up Resolution 807 (1993) and to further extend the mandate of UNPROFOR. The two resolutions, according to France, were based on the same priority considerations, including a guarantee of better security for the Force, for which they had recourse to Chapter VII of the Charter.[41] The new resolution's last preambular paragraph reads essentially the same as that of Resolution 807 (1993), except for an addition: "Determined to ensure the security of UNPROFOR and its freedom of movement for all its missions, and *to these ends* acting under Chapter VII of the Charter of the United Nations, . . . " [emphasis added].

## OPERATIONS WITH MILITARY ENFORCEMENT POWER

The third and undoubtedly most important implication of the reference to Chapter VII in peacekeeping resolutions is that it has authorized, though sometimes implicitly, the U.N. personnel to use force beyond self-defense. This also constitutes the most revolutionary feature of the post–Cold War peacekeeping operations.

The first and most conspicuous such occasion came with Security Council Resolution 814 of March 26, 1993, which expanded the size and mandate of the U.N. Operation in Somalia (UNOSOM) and thus established UNOSOM-II in accordance with the recommendations contained in the Secretary-General's report. In the report, he pointed out that, after the operations of the Unified Task Force (UNITAF), the security threat to the United Nations and its agencies was still high, and disarmament was far from complete. Based on such an assessment and also proceeding from his firm view that the mandate of UNOSOM-II must include disarmament, the Secretary-General, after listing several military tasks as the possible mandate for UNOSOM-II (e.g., control of heavy weapons, seizure of small arms, and neutralization of armed elements), recommended that UNOSOM-II be endowed with "enforcement powers under Chapter VII of the Charter" in order to implement the new mandate.[42] As the Secretary-General mentioned in the report, UNOSOM-II was indeed "the first operation of this kind."[43]

Although far less apparent, a somewhat similar development seems to be taking place in the former Yugoslavia. Resolution 836 of June 4, 1993, extended the mandate for UNPROFOR in order to enable it, *inter alia*, to deter attacks against the "safe areas" in Bosnia and Herzegovina. The "safe areas" are those areas in Bosnia where fighting has been particularly intense and the humanitarian situation has continued to deteriorate, and which, the Security Council has demanded, should thus be free from any armed attack or any other hostile act.[44] The resolution specifically authorized UNPROFOR in Bosnia, "acting in self-defence, to take the necessary measures, including the use of force, in reply to bombardments against the safe areas . . . or to armed incursion into them or in the event of any deliberate obstruction in or around those areas to the freedom of movement of UNPROFOR or of protected humanitarian convoys" (see paragraph 9).[45]

It may be said that the U.N. authorization in this case remains within the scope of self-defense, particularly in light of the explicit reference to "self-defence" in the resolution itself. It is, however, equally worth mentioning that the resolution also contains the following expression: "take the necessary measures, including the use of force," which bears a close resemblance to the wording of a resolution authorizing a military-enforcement action. Did Resolution 836 (1993) authorize the use of force by UNPROFOR in situations other than traditional self-defense?

The concept of self-defense in peacekeeping has traditionally meant something different from what it means for a sovereign state. According to the typical guidelines for traditional peacekeeping operations, the U.N. force will not use force except in self-defense; and self-defense here would include "resistance to attempts by forceful means to prevent it from discharging its duties under the mandate of the Security Council."[46] This means that peacekeepers may use force against armed persons who attempt to disturb the peacekeeping activities *without* involving an actual armed attack. But, referring to the detailed examples described in the guidelines for peacekeeping operations, their use of force still remains restricted to the situations where U.N. personnel are directly affected in one way or another.[47] In any case, it should be noted that there was a qualitative difference between the tasks of UNOSOM-II under Resolution 814 (1993) and those of UNPROFOR under Resolution 836 (1993); the former being actively to disarm the local clan militias, while the latter passively to respond to the bombardments or deliberate obstructions by the local parties.

In Resolution 836 (1993), however, the use of force was authorized in response to bombardments against the "safe areas," not UNPROFOR itself; to armed incursions into those areas, and in the event of any deliberate obstruction to the freedom of movement not only of UNPROFOR but also of "protected humanitarian convoys." This exhibits a slight but meaningful difference from the traditional concept of self-defense in peacekeeping. It may safely be said that U.N. authorization of the use of force in Resolution 836 (1993), although stopping short of conveying enforcement power,[48] falls in between that of UNOSOM-II and that of traditional peacekeeping. Or, to make more of a reference to "self-defence" in the resolution, it may be that the concept of self-defense has been enlarged in this case beyond its traditional meaning.[49]

One must admit that there was, among traditional peacekeeping operations, one exception in which the use of force was permitted beyond self-defense. In the early 1960s, when ONUC performed its functions in Central Africa, the Security Council twice adopted a resolution to authorize the use of force. The original mandate for ONUC stated, regarding the application of force by the peacekeepers, that the military units would be entitled to act only in self-defense.[50] Responding to the killing of Congolese leaders, including Prime Minister Patrice Lumumba, however, the United Nations, by Security Council Resolution 161 of February 21, 1961, urged ONUC to take all appropriate measures, including the use of force, if necessary (though as a last resort), to prevent the occurrence of a civil war in the Congo. ONUC actually used force in April to stop the civil war in Katanga, which was a secessionist province of the Congo.

Again in Resolution 169 of November 24, 1961, the Security Council, in demanding the end of the "illegal" secessionist activities in Katanga, authorized the Secretary-General to take vigorous action, including the use of the requisite measure of force, if necessary, for the immediate apprehension, detention, and/or deportation of all foreign military personnel not under the U.N. command and mercenaries. Fighting took place the next month. Although opinions are divided as to whether the former resolution authorized the use of force beyond self-defense, it would surely be difficult to consider the use of force in the latter context as self-defense.[51]

Despite all this, one should not overlook one important distinction between the use of force by ONUC and that by UNOSOM-II. While, in Somalia, the U.N. military might has been directed against the Somali people themselves, ONUC resorted to the use of force only to evacuate foreign troops and mercenaries. Ralph Bunche, then Under-Secretary-General, categorically declined the U.S. proposal to attack the Congolese National Army, his aim being always to avoid a situation in which the U.N. soldiers might be forced to shoot at the Congolese.[52]

# PEACEKEEPING UNDER CHAPTER VII: AN ASSESSMENT

Some of the "second generation" peacekeeping operations established under Chapter VII of the U.N. Charter may be designated as operations under "Chapter VI¾."[53] For, notwithstanding the explicit reference to "Chapter VII," they encompass both traditional peacekeeping activities under "Chapter VI½" and (quasi-) enforcement elements under "Chapter VII." Specifically, operations for which Chapter VII is rightly invoked and which really deserve the designation are, as would be apparent from the discussions above, those set up without the consent of the host state and/or authorization to use force beyond self-defense. The questions that one might ask regarding such operations are whether they are really peacekeeping and whether they are desirable for the purpose of maintaining international peace and security.

## ARE THEY PEACEKEEPING?

The answer to the first question would almost exclusively depend on how one defines peacekeeping and what one considers to be the essential characteristics that distinguish it from other U.N. peace activities. Although some principles guiding the establishment and performance of a peacekeeping operation have been developed through practice, the United Nations has *officially* formulated no definition or criteria for U.N. peacekeeping. Without U.N. guidance, the efforts to seek the answer to the question become futile or at least quite subjective.

Nonetheless, by referring to the U.N. documents, one can at least identify the views of the United Nations or its secretariat. It should be noted in this regard that there is a small but still important difference between the two definitions of "peacekeeping" recently put forward by the Secretary-General on different occasions.

In *An Agenda for Peace*, peacekeeping was defined as "the deployment of a United Nations presence in the field, *hitherto* with the consent of all the parties concerned, normally involving United Nations military and/or police personnel and frequently civilians as well" [emphasis added]. However, in one of his latest reports on peacekeeping, titled "Improving the Capacity of the United Nations for Peacekeeping," the word "hitherto" was omitted in the corresponding definition of peacekeeping, and "the consent of the parties" is simply mentioned.[54] Such a development arguably represents a change in the Secretary-General's perception of peacekeeping. That is, in mid-1992, he may have considered that the local consent required of traditional peacekeeping should not necessarily be made an operational *sine qua non* for the post–Cold War operations;[55] but after experiencing a new type of U.N. operation for one year, notably in Somalia, he might have changed his perception and finally recognized the importance of the consent and cooperation of the parties concerned to the success of the operation. If so, it might follow that U.N. operations without the consent of the parties concerned should not be considered to be peacekeeping operations.

Yet U.N. operations without local consent, such as UNIKOM and UNOSOM-II, continue to be placed among peacekeeping operations in the U.N. documents.[56] Of course, they may be there for the sake of simple continuation of previous activities of the same name (the case of UNOSOM-II). But it is also a fact that in terms of the entrusted missions, some of them do not differ from traditional peacekeeping (as in the case of UNIKOM). As such, they may be entitled to claim a place in U.N. documents side-by-side with other peacekeeping operations. The members of the Security Council and of the General Assembly's Special Committee on Peacekeeping Operations seem to accept the concept that peacekeeping operations may not require the consent of the host state.[57]

In the case of operations with enforcement power (or power to use force beyond self-defense), however, the missions are so different from those for traditional peacekeeping that the operations may be viewed as enforcement measures themselves and no longer as part of peacekeeping.[58] Nevertheless, such operations as UNO-SOM-II and UNPROFOR are likewise listed in the U.N. documents

as peacekeeping. This is perhaps from similar considerations discussed above. UNPROFOR, for instance, was originally established
in 1992 purely for traditional peacekeeping purposes, and the normal rules for the bearing and use of arms in peacekeeping applied;[59]
but its mandate has been enlarged several times by Council resolutions, including Resolution 836 (1993), which authorized UNPRO-
FOR in Bosnia to use force beyond self-defense. Nonetheless,
UNPROFOR in Bosnia, with such a different mandate, still constitutes a part of UNPROFOR and mainly performs traditional peacekeeping functions.

In any case, the Security Council seems to endorse the idea
of peacekeeping with enforcement power or power to use force
beyond self-defense as well. After a special meeting devoted to
*An Agenda for Peace*, the Security Council recommended several
operational principles guiding U.N. "peacekeeping" operations,
including the right of the Security Council to authorize "all means
necessary for United Nations forces to carry out their mandate,"
in addition to the inherent right of U.N. forces to take measures
for self-defense.[60]

Thus the Security Council, the General Assembly's Special
Committee on Peacekeeping Operations, and the secretariat seem
to regard as peacekeeping those operations established without
local consent or endowed with enforcement powers. Of course,
there is no absolute need to conclude that they are peacekeeping,
nor is it beyond a shadow of question to do so. However, it is also
difficult to declare that the classification by the secretariat is false,
given the absence of an official U.N. definition of peacekeeping.

## ARE THEY DESIRABLE?

Irrespective of the categorization, whether these new-wave U.N.
operations are desirable for the purpose of maintaining international peace and security is another question. Here, the focus should
be placed on the situations in Bosnia and Somalia, over which
Secretary-General Boutros-Ghali continues to express grave concern. In both cases the peacekeepers operating in these countries
have been vested with enforcement power or the power to use force
beyond self-defense, *and* they are operating without necessarily the
full consent or support of the parties concerned.[61] In terms of the
nature of the local situation, too, there are at least three more
elements common to both countries, and these elements seem to

have a somewhat close bearing not only on the way the United Nations has responded to the situation but also on the results it has brought about.

First of all, both countries are essentially in civil war–type situations. In a civil war, leaders of local factions are not always responsive to the demands of the international community for adherence to agreements and acceptance of U.N. operations; and it is often more difficult to obtain their consent to and cooperation with the U.N. presence than it is in ordinary state-to-state conflict situations. In Bosnia, the full deployment of UNPROFOR in the republic by Resolution 776 (1992) was reportedly authorized without clear consent from the parties concerned.[62]

The situation was far more puzzling in Somalia. When UNOSOM-II was set up and even before that, there was no effectively functioning government in the country and there were, instead, more than a dozen local factions competing with one another.[63] Under these circumstances, it is simply impossible even to identify the parties whose consent is legally necessary to set up a peacekeeping operation, and the invocation of Chapter VII in this case may have been an inevitability.

Problems in peacekeeping in a civil war are not limited to those of securing the necessary consent. They also involve another fundamental principle of peacekeeping, which is the principle of impartiality. Since the warring factions are struggling for legitimacy in a civil war, they are quite sensitive to U.N. behavior in terms of whether the United Nations is on their side or on the other. At the same time, each of the competing factions tends to try to resolve the pending issues in its favor, sometimes even to the frustration of the peacekeepers. Consequently, it becomes extremely difficult for the peacekeepers to remain neutral among the factions. In Bosnia, in spite of the fact noted in the next paragraph, each warring side has reportedly perceived the peacekeepers as favoring its enemy.[64] In a civil war context, we should always remember and heed Secretary-General Dag Hammarskjöld's weighty warning, given as early as 1958, that it is extremely difficult for a U.N. force to operate in an internal conflict without soon becoming a party to the conflict.[65]

Secondly, in both Bosnia and Somalia, enforcement activities have targeted some particular group in each country. As regards Bosnia, U.N. enforcement measures have been aimed primarily at the Bosnian Serbs and the Federal Republic of Yugoslavia (Serbia and Montenegro), which support their Bosnian brothers. Security Council Resolution 757 of May 30, 1992, imposed a general trade embargo on the Federal Republic of Yugoslavia; and Resolution 770 of August 13, 1992 (paragraph 2), called upon states, under Chapter VII, to take all measures necessary to facilitate the delivery of humanitarian assistance in Bosnia, which has been obstructed primarily by the local Serbs. The latter resolution, although not implemented as such in reality,[66] is interpreted to have authorized the use of force to accomplish the humanitarian delivery. It was under such circumstances that, by Council Resolution 776 of September 14, 1992, the U.N. peacekeepers were deployed throughout the Republic of Bosnia and Herzegovina to support and protect the humanitarian relief operations by the U.N. High Commissioner for Refugees.

In Somalia, the situation seemed essentially the same. U.N. enforcement measures targeted, as a consequence, the faction headed by General Mohammed Farah Aidid. Security Council Resolution 733 of January 23, 1992, unanimously decreed "a general and complete embargo on all deliveries of weapons and military equipment to Somalia," responding to the request of the "Somali government" (in fact, a strong Somali faction fighting against Aidid) to discuss the issue and with its implicit approval.[67] In the meantime, the other strong faction in Somalia headed by General Aidid was hostile to the United Nations: It not only rejected a U.N. proposed ceasefire in Mogadishu (to which all the other factions agreed) in early 1992, but it also declined the deployment of UNO-SOM (which had been approved by the Security Council in April) until the fall of 1992.[68] Resolution 794 of December 3, 1992, which authorized member states to use "all necessary means" to establish a secure environment for humanitarian relief operations in Somalia, was not explicitly directed at the Aidid faction. Nevertheless, the resolution, which placed all the factions on an equal footing, could have been interpreted by the Aidid faction, by far the biggest, to be in effect detrimental to its interests. After the multinational operations carried out by UNITAF in accordance with this resolution, UNOSOM-II undertook both peacekeeping and peace-enforcement tasks pursuant to Resolution 814 of March 26, 1993. In fact, UNOSOM-II took over what had been left unfinished by UNITAF coalition forces.[69]

The United Nations, in these cases, was neither impartial nor neutral among warring factions from the outset, for whatever reasons the peacekeepers were deployed. Indeed, it almost became a full-fledged party to the internal conflict and, as such, could no longer be eligible to be a neutral intermediary to resolve the underlying problems, even on a temporary basis. Here, the United Nations falls into a dilemma of at once being the center of "neutral" peacekeeping and being too closely associated with collective enforcement that is conceptually antithetical to the neutral and impartial approach expected of peacekeeping.

The same is true of any case in which the United Nations conducts peacekeeping and, at the same time, authorizes regional agencies to use force—"a disciplinary measure", so to speak—against those parties attacking the peacekeepers or defying the agencies' orders. In Bosnia, for instance, the United Nations seems to have become an enemy to the Bosnian Serbs when NATO made its first-ever air attacks on ground targets (Serbs) around Gorazde on April 10 and 11, 1994, and then around Sarajevo on August 5 and September 22, 1994, in accordance with Resolution 836 (1993).[70] Serbs and their armored vehicles were attacked by reason of their continued offensive against Gorazde in April, their capture of heavy weapons under the U.N. control in August, and their attacks on UNPROFOR personnel in September. After the first series of NATO attacks in April, the Bosnian Serb leader, Radovan Karadzic, reportedly notified the U.N. Secretary-General that he was now forced to regard UNPROFOR in Bosnia as an enemy force; by the same token, he warned that, after the September air strike, "If there are going to be more air strikes, then there is going to be war between us and the international community."[71] This is not saying that the air strikes were themselves an inappropriate measure in these cases; but it is simply saying that the combination of peacekeeping and peace enforcement at one time was counter-productive.

In this connection, one should recall that the United Nations took a quite discreet, truly commendable approach in dealing with the Cambodia conflict. It imposed an oil embargo upon the Khmer Rouge–controlled areas not through Chapter VII of the U.N. Charter but as a measure within the framework of the Agreement of a Comprehensive Political Settlement of the Cambodia Conflict, to which the faction was a party.[72] This without doubt contributed to the maintenance of the neutrality of UNTAC to the extent possible, while enabling the United Nations to carry out the necessary steps.

The third feature common to the situations in Bosnia and Somalia is that the peacekeepers were sent while the hostilities were still going on. When UNPROFOR was deployed in Bosnia and Herzegovina, no real ceasefire was in place. In Somalia, too, when the Secretary-General proposed a transition from UNITAF to UNOSOM-II, a secure environment had not yet been established and incidents of violence continued to occur.[73] It is because of this fact that the United Nations has been requested to provide assistance to protect and ensure the secure delivery of humanitarian supplies to the areas of need.

Assuming that a peacekeeping operation is an activity to "keep peace," there should be at least some kind of "peace" to be kept. As was discussed earlier, the concept of "peace" in peacekeeping is relatively limited in scope, covering a period of temporary cessation of hostilities during an armed conflict. In the cases of Bosnia and Somalia, however, there did not even exist such limited peace; on the contrary, there continued to be violent military actions among a number of hostile parties. As such, conditions were not yet ripe for launching a peacekeeping operation there. This is precisely why the Security Council had to decide to endow the peacekeepers with the authority to use force beyond self-defense or enforcement powers.

However, a peacekeeping operation with enforcement power will almost inevitably amount to an awkward half-measure both for peacekeeping and peace enforcement. On the one hand, peacekeepers with enforcement power would no longer be impartial among parties to the conflict and could not perform what is expected of a neutral U.N. force. Even for traditional peacekeepers, it is sometimes difficult and may be close to impossible to remain fully impartial and neutral;[74] and that "intended" impartiality does not always lead to "perceived" impartiality in effect. Unlike traditional peacekeeping operations, a peacekeeping operation with enforcement power cannot, by its nature, play an impartial role. The same is true of the peacekeeping operations with the power to use force beyond self-defense but a degree of power less than enforcement.

On the other hand, a military enforcement action generally requires an overwhelming number of fighting units equipped sufficiently with offensive heavy weapons as well as reliable and capable command and control over the multinational operation, which usually is not accompanied by peacekeeping operations. As a result, requiring a peacekeeping force to conduct an enforcement action could expose its personnel to great danger. An operation with peacekeeping and peace-enforcement missions mixed up thus seems in most cases to prove fruitless at the end of the day; or worse, it may aggravate the situation by adding another uncertain element to an already complicated equation.

To sum up, Bosnia and Somalia have confronted the United Nations with the worst conceivable situation: The United Nations has to carry out its tasks impartially—at least in part—in a civil war where it cannot be regarded as neutral from the outset. Against this backdrop, peacekeeping may not have been the appropriate measure to be taken to respond to the situation in Bosnia.[75] In Somalia, peacekeeping activities were resumed improperly in both timing and manner, and the vesting of enforcement power in the peacekeepers resulted in further deterioration of the situation. It is essential that the United Nations learn lessons from these experiences, for the protracted internal conflicts with humanitarian needs are not exceptions but, indeed, represent the surging phenomenon in the post–Cold War era, and the United Nations will increasingly be called upon to extend assistance.[76]

## CONCLUSIONS

Since the end of the Cold War, the United Nations has embarked upon new enterprises for the maintenance of international peace and security. This is particularly visible in the field of peacekeeping, which has been needed as a result of the worldwide outbreak of ethnic conflicts and secessionist movements unleashed by the collapse of a global order based on the Cold War confrontation. The increased need for peacekeeping has surprised some observers, since peacekeeping operations are an illegitimate child of the Cold War and it might have been thought that they would disappear with the end of the superpower rivalry that brought them into being. On the contrary, we see, as Marrack Goulding aptly puts it, "the forced development of peacekeeping" today.[77]

At the same time, the United Nations now suffers from tremendous difficulties in its performance, manpower, equipment, finance, and administration for peacekeeping, and to that extent its credibility as the world peace organization is also undermined. This situation may well have been caused by the fact that the United Nations has had to respond swiftly to the rapidly growing number of requests for assistance without having either the time or the capacity to construct a sound strategy for each case.[78] True as this explanation may be, the United Nations now stands at a real watershed in its peacekeeping history, and it is high time to learn from the mistakes of the past.

The first issue to be addressed is overcommitment and overstretch. The United Nations has replied to most of the major post–Cold War conflicts by sending peacekeepers. The result is a notorious financial crisis, shortages of manpower and equipment, and disorder at the secretariat. U.N. forces could not always accomplish their mandated missions, and they even worsened the situation in some cases. For the restoration of U.N. credibility, which is key to sustaining international peace and security in the long run, it would be "better to have a few successes than to seek many successes with some gross failures" and, in some cases, "better nothing than making the situation worse." The United Nations need not respond to unrealistic, inflated expectations. This is, of course, not to advocate a negative approach, but, rather, to recommend that it take a *selective approach* to different types of conflicts that may occur in various parts of the globe, considering in particular the aptitude and capabilities of the United Nations in peacekeeping for dealing with the given conflict and whether the parties concerned have the intention and ability themselves to settle the dispute.

In this context, it may be worth exploring whether the United Nations could more often utilize regional organizations for peacekeeping purposes.[79] On the peacemaking front, the U.N. Charter provides that the Security Council should encourage the development of pacific settlement of local disputes through regional arrangements or regional agencies (Article 52). This also seems to apply to peacekeeping. After all, states must have a genuine interest in keeping peace in their neighborhood: they know the region best and would be most directly affected by adverse outcomes. Yet, the present arrangements of most regional organizations for peacekeeping are undoubtedly feeble and would certainly require a drastic amplification of their capabilities in this field before they could be utilized by the United Nations. It goes without saying that such regional peacekeepers should abide by the traditional peacekeeping principles.

Secondly, there need be some reconstruction of U.N. peace efforts. As has been discussed, the recent U.N. peace activities are dominated by a contemporaneous, composite approach: peace-keeping combined with other peace-related functions. While peacekeeping with preventive diplomacy or peace building combined—still largely under the traditional peacekeeping principles—has attained a general success so far, peacekeeping vested with peace-enforcement power (or power to use force beyond self-defense)—scarcely under such principles—has incurred, bluntly put, a disastrous blow or at least has confronted itself with great difficulties. The latter attempt was, indeed, to try to do what is impossible from the beginning. Peacekeeping is a non-partisan and non-enforcing activity, and this very nature is the source of its strength and authority and thus its successes. On the other hand, peace enforcement is an activity whereby the United Nations forcibly applies sanctions against a selected wrongdoer and against its will; and as such, it has also achieved a general success so far, though not often. However, these two activities are inherently incompatible with one another, and hence their combination in one single operation would inevitably involve an internal contradiction and would be in all probability destined to fail.[80] In order not to repeat the recent failures, it would be essential to maintain a *separate approach* to the two U.N. peace operations—perhaps based on such criteria as whether an effective ceasefire is established and whether there is enough consent and cooperation among the parties concerned.

With the above in mind, it comes as no surprise that the Security Council decided in early 1994 to abandon the peace-enforcement elements of the U.N. operation in Somalia.[81] Also relevant here is the fact that the Security Council later in the same year decided not to endow peacekeepers of the U.N. Assistance Mission for Rwanda with enforcement powers under Chapter VII, which had been proposed by the Secretary-General in his report as one of the options to be considered by the Security Council.[82] It is still to be determined, however, whether these instances mean that the United Nations has started to reconsider its tendency to resort to Chapter VII too easily in peacekeeping.

Thirdly, once the United Nations, faced with a resurrection of major hostilities or otherwise, chooses to cross the "impartiality divide" from peacekeeping to peace enforcement, it should execute the military-enforcement measure with decisive force and in a decisive manner without hesitation. In Bosnia, however, quite the opposite seems to have happened. The local Serb forces took advantage of the divergence of opinion between the United States and its West European allies as to whether to use airpower against the Serbs if they harmed U.N. personnel. The latter countries, which have contributed their contingents to UNPROFOR, were concerned about their troops' safety and rejected the U.S. idea. It is said that London's repeated public display of concern for the safety of its UNPROFOR contingent emboldened the Bosnian Serbs and encouraged them to threaten British and other U.N. forces as a way to derail Western attempts to interfere with their activities.[83] Although not a peace-enforcement case, this episode tells us, as a bad example, how important it is for the United Nations to make the conflicting parties aware of its determination to use force in unmistakable terms, once it has decided to resort to military peace enforcement.

An indomitable resolve for peace enforcement may serve as an effective instrument in a peacekeeping context as well. If, for instance, peacekeepers are attacked in a systematic way or if major violence recurs after their deployment, the United Nations could bring pressure on the parties in question by withdrawing or hinting at a withdrawal of the peacekeepers, thus sending a message to the parties that U.N. military-enforcement action may be forthcoming. In order for the message to be credible, the United Nations must be equipped with a firm determination to resort to enforcement as well as resources that would back up the determination.

In this connection, one may recall that UNIKOM is the only peacekeeping operation under Chapter VII that has not suffered from the serious difficulties encountered in the other cases. Unlike UNPROFOR and UNOSOM-II, UNIKOM was neither deployed in a civil war nor given military-enforcement powers under Chapter VII. These facts have undoubtedly contributed to its relative success to date. But it should not be overlooked that major hostile actions by Iraq against UNIKOM would surely lead to the coalition powers' resumed military enforcement against Iraq, and that such a possibility has also contributed to deter Iraqi actions. Thus, a firm determination to use military enforcement, backed by ample resources, could promote effective and successful peacekeeping as well.

The problem is that the United Nations is not always assured of the timely provision of the necessary resources for military enforcement from its member states. Concluding a "special agreement," as foreseen in Article 43 of the Charter, has been advocated as a means to obtain the assurances, but it seems unlikely, though not impossible, to think about its early realization at this stage. Here, too, a regional approach might possibly be a way out. In this connection, NATO's recent experiences in helping carry out the Security Council decisions in Bosnia warrant both a careful and an in-depth examination. Independently of the results, however, it should always be kept in mind that the success of the United Nations in the field of maintaining international peace and security will, as in other fields, largely depend on the will of its member states. Ultimately, an international organization cannot do more than its members are prepared to take the pains to accomplish, and the United Nations is no exception to this rule.

## NOTES

[1] Since May 1990, there have been only two vetoes cast in the Security Council: on May 11, 1993, and December 2, 1994, by the Russian Federation on the questions of mandatory financing for the U.N. Peacekeeping Force in Cyprus and the strengthening of economic sanctions against the Federal Republic of Yugoslavia, respectively.

[2] S/23500, January 31, 1992, p. 3.

[3] A/47/277–S/24111, June 17, 1992 (hereafter cited as *An Agenda for Peace*).

[4] A/48/403–S/26450, March 14, 1994, para. 67.

[5] Brian Urquhart, "Beyond the 'Sheriff's Posse'," *Survival* 32:3 (May/June 1990), p. 196. Promptly on taking office, Secretary-General Boutros-Ghali implemented a major simplification of the administrative structure of the secretariat, resulting in the consolidation of five former departments and offices into a new Department of Political Affairs and the creation of three other new departments, including the "Department of Peacekeeping Operations." *UN Chronicle* 29:2 (June 1992), p. 3.

[6] Some authors incorrectly use the term "peacemaking" to mean peace enforcement. See, e.g., Wendell Gordon, *The United Nations at the Crossroads of Reform* (M.E. Sharpe, 1994), pp. 36, 38, 224ff. This is perhaps because Secretary-General Boutros-Ghali in *An Agenda for Peace* discussed matters related to U.N. military sanctions under the heading of "Peacemaking." See *An Agenda for Peace*, paras. 42, 43. There was no heading of "Peace enforcement" in that report. The Secretary-General later put the concept of "peace enforcement" in his report along with other concepts already contained in *An Agenda for Peace*. A/48/403–S/26450, para. 4. See also Boutros Boutros-Ghali, *Report on the Work of the Organization from the Forty-seventh to the Forty-eighth Session of the General Assembly*, September 1993, para. 278.

[7] Cf. A/48/403–S/26450, para. 4(d). Some authors, however, tend to emphasize the difference between peace enforcement and Article 42 enforcement as follows: The former is a provisional measure taken without prejudice to the position of any of the parties, while the latter is directed against an aggressor. See James S. Sutterlin, *Military Force in the Service of Peace*, Aurora Papers 18 (Canadian Centre for Global Security, 1993), pp. 21–22, 28.

[8] *The Blue Helmets: A Review of United Nations Peace-Keeping*, 2nd ed. (United Nations, 1990), p. 5. The so-called "implied powers" of the United Nations are

also referred to as a basis for U.N. peacekeeping operations. Ibid. As its note states, though, this publication is not a formal report of the United Nations.

[9]See "United Nations Emergency Force: Summary Study of the Experience Derived from the Establishment and Operation of the Force," A/3943, October 9, 1958, paras. 154–193, esp. paras. 155, 160, 166, 167, 179. The "Summary Study" was not formally approved by the U.N. General Assembly. Robert C.R. Siekmann, *National Contingents in United Nations Peace-Keeping Forces* (Nijhoff, 1992), p. 7.

[10]*An Agenda for Peace*, para. 20.

[11]Oscar Schachter, "The Uses of Law in International Peace-keeping," *Virginia Law Review*, Vol. 50 (1964), pp. 1105–106.

[12]Professor Malitza argues that the state of non-belligerency is inadequately called "peace" in peacekeeping operations. Mircea Malitza, "The Improvement of Effectiveness of United Nations Peacekeeping Operations," in UNITAR, *The United Nations and the Maintenance of International Peace and Security* (Nijhoff, 1987), p. 239.

[13]For the recent cases where the concept of a "threat to the peace" was invoked, see Helmut Freudenschuβ, "Article 39 of the UN Charter Revisited: Threats to the Peace and the Recent Practice of the UN Security Council," *Australian Journal of Public and International Law* 46:1 (1993), pp. 1–39. See also Ruth Gordon, "United Nations Intervention in Internal Conflicts: Iraq, Somalia, and Beyond," *Michigan Journal of International Law* 15:2 (Winter 1994), pp. 519–89.

[14]The term "preventive diplomacy" carries manifold meanings. It was first introduced by former Secretary-General Dag Hammarskjöld, who used the term to mean what is now known as peacekeeping. See "Introduction to the Annual Report of the Secretary-General on the Work of the Organization, June 16, 1959–June 15, 1960," A/4390/Add. 1, 1960, p. 4. In his *An Agenda for Peace*, Secretary-General Boutros-Ghali, it is said, infused a new life into the elusive and undefined concept of preventive diplomacy. See Boutros-Ghali, *Report on the Work of the Organization*, September 1993, para. 279.

[15]According to a U.N. list, thirteen peacekeeping operations were established between 1948 and 1978. After UNIFIL of March 1978, there had been no new peacekeeping operations set up for ten years until UNGOMAP of April 1988. Since 1988, the United Nations has launched twenty new operations (as of November 1993). *United Nations Peace-Keeping Operations: Information Notes—1993, Update No. 2*, DPI/1306/Rev. 2, November 1993.

[16]Wiseman stresses the discontinuities during the "first generation" era: "the Nascent Period" of 1946–1956, "the Assertive Period" of 1956–1967, and "the Resurgent Period" of 1973–78. Henry Wiseman, "The United Nations and International Peacekeeping: A Comparative Analysis," in UNITAR, *The United Nations and the Maintenance of International Peace and Security*, pp. 263–309.

[17]The expression "second generation" peacekeeping operations is gaining currency. David Ruzié, "Maintaining, Building and Enforcing Peace: A Legal Perspective," *UNIDIR Newsletter*, No. 24 (December 1993), p. 13.

[18]See, e.g., W. Michael Reisman, "Peacemaking," *Yale Journal of International Law* 18:1 (Winter 1993), p. 415; Indar Jit Rikhye, *Strengthening UN Peacekeeping* (U.S. Institute of Peace, 1992), p. 12; and "The Future of Peacekeeping," in Indar Jit Rikhye and Kjell Skjelsbaek, eds., *The United Nations and Peacekeeping* (Macmillan, 1990), p. 173. On difficulties with UNIFIL's withdrawal, see Marianne

Heiberg, "Peacekeepers and Local Populations: Some Comments on UNIFIL," in ibid., pp. 155–56.

[19]S/12636, April 10, 1978 (Five-Party Proposal for a Settlement of the Namibian Situation); S/12827, August 29, 1978 (Secretary-General's Report on the Implementation of the Five-Party Proposal). See also Virginia Page Fortna, "United Nations Transition Assistance Group," in William J. Durch, ed., *The Evolution of UN Peacekeeping: Case Studies and Comparative Analysis* (St. Martin's Press, 1993), p. 355.

[20]United Nations, *Agreements on a Comprehensive Political Settlement of the Cambodian Conflict, Paris, 23 October 1991*. In the main agreement, "all powers necessary to ensure the implementation of this Agreement" was delegated to the United Nations (Article 6).

[21]Robert C.R. Siekmann, *Basic Documents on United Nations and Related Peace-Keeping Forces*, 2nd ed. (Nijhoff, 1989), pp. 137–141.

[22]Such an idea had already been put forward before *An Agenda for Peace*. See, e.g., E. Suy, "Legal Aspects of UN Peace-Keeping Operations," *Netherlands International Law Review* 35:3 (1988), p. 320; Nikolai B. Krylov, "International Peacekeeping and Enforcement After the Cold War," in Lori Fisler Damrosch and David J. Scheffer, eds., *Law and Force in the New International Order* (Westview Press, 1991), p. 98; and A/47/253, June 4, 1992, para. 26.

[23]*An Agenda for Peace*, paras. 31–32.

[24]See Thomas G. Weiss, "New Challenges for UN Military Operations: Implementing an Agenda for Peace," *Washington Quarterly* 16:1 (Winter 1993), p. 59.

[25]A/6730/Add. 3, June 26, 1967, para. 34. See also Maurice Flory, "Le retrait de la Force d'urgence des Nations Unies," *Annuaire Français de Droit International*, tome 14 (1968), pp. 377–388.

[26]Egypt's action was not motivated by pure bellicosity, but by an aspiration to maintain its prestige in the Arab world. It had in fact been taunted by other Arab countries with sitting safely behind the U.N. Force and making bellicose propaganda. See M.D. Donelan and M.J. Grieve, *International Disputes: Case Histories 1945–1970* (Europa Pub., 1973), pp. 269–73.

[27]A/6730/Add. 3, op cit., para. 92.

[28]See, ibid., paras. 83–86, 89. One way of avoiding the U.N. withdrawal upon unilateral decision by Egypt would have been, as the General Assembly proposed in Resolution 1125 (XI) of February 2, 1957, to allow a U.N. presence on the Israeli side of the demarcation line as well. Israel, however, did not accept that proposal, keeping the position expressed before that it would not agree to the stationing of a foreign force, no matter how called, in its territory or its occupied territories.

[29]S/4113, November 17, 1958, p. 1.

[30]Marrack Goulding, "The Evolution of United Nations Peacekeeping," *International Affairs* (London) 69:3 (July 1993), p. 458. However, the normal pattern is that all parties fail, to a greater or lesser extent, to comply perfectly with the agreement they have signed. Ibid.

[31]Yasushi Akashi, the then Special Representative of the Secretary-General for Cambodia, pointed out in an interview with a Japanese newspaper that the Cambodian success was made possible by pursuing "a soft peace-keeping operation placing emphasis on diplomacy rather than force, and persuasion rather than coercion." *Yomiuri Shinbun*, July 27, 1993.

[32]The mandate and characteristics of UNPROFOR cannot be described in plain terms. They are different from one Republic of the former Yugoslavia to another (Croatia, Bosnia and Herzegovina, and Macedonia) and have evolved over time.

[33]During the first several weeks, though, some infantry units were deployed to provide initial security. Resolution 806 of February 5, 1993, extended UNIKOM's terms of reference to include the "capacity to take physical action" to prevent violations of the DMZ and of the newly demarcated boundary between Iraq and Kuwait. The authorization of the use of force is, however, within the limits of self-defense and not for enforcement action. S/25123, January 18, 1993, paras. 5, 10. This was a U.N. reaction to a series of border incidents in January 1993, including Iraq's unauthorized retrieval of missiles and other military equipment from Kuwaiti territory.

[34]Op cit., Durch, "The Iraq-Kuwait Observation Mission," p. 269.

[35]S/25354, March 3, 1993, para. 97.

[36]Security Council Resolution 743 (1992) establishing UNPROFOR recalled "Article 25 of the UN Charter" (providing for the obligatory nature of the Council "decisions") in a preambular paragraph, and "decide[d]" to establish UNPROFOR. Some authors therefore suggest that "the Security Council might actually require the states involved to accept the continued presence of peacekeeping forces. . ., whether they wished this or not." Adam Roberts, "Humanitarian War: Military Intervention and Human Rights," *International Affairs* (London) 69:3 (July 1993), p. 442. However in establishing peacekeeping operations, the Security Council has always "decided" their establishment with the exception of only UNFICYP; and such decisions, based on the prior consent of the host state, merely signify that the host state is bound to accept the peacekeepers for the period established and that in principle it is not entitled to ask for their withdrawal before the term expires. Cf. Antonietta Di Blase, "The Role of the Host State's Consent with Regard to Non-Coercive Actions by the United Nations," in A. Cassese, ed., *United Nations Peace-Keeping: Legal Essays* (Sijthoff & Noordhoff, 1978), p. 75. For the drafting process of Resolution 743 (1992), with particular reference to the duration of the term see Freudenschuβ, "Article 39 of the UN Charter Revisited," op cit., pp. 13–14.

[37]The "United Nations Protected Areas (UNPAs)" are those areas in Croatia designated for the deployment of UNPROFOR where Serbs constitute the majority or a substantial minority of the population and inter-communal tensions have led to armed conflict in the recent past. There are other ares in Croatia, called "pink zones," that are populated largely by Serbs but are outside the agreed UNPA boundaries. Local Serb leaders have pressed strongly for the "pink zones" to be included in the UNPA, but Croatian authorities resisted, equally strongly, any change in the UNPA boundaries. Neither the UNPAs nor the "pink zones" are under Croatian control. See S/23280, December 11, 1991, Annex III (UN peace-keeping plan in Croatia), para. 8; *The United Nations and the Situation in the Former Yugoslavia*, DPI/1312/Rev. 1, June 1993, pp. 3–4.

[38]The Croatian offensive took place out of impatience with the slow progress of negotiations with respect to various economic facilities in and adjacent to the UNPAs and the "pink zones." For details of situations leading to the adoption of the resolution, see S/25264, February 10, 1993, paras. 12–17.

[39]S/PV.3174, February 19, 1993, pp. 13–15.

[40]Ibid., pp. 16, 21.

[41]S/PV.3189, March 30, 1993, pp. 3–4.

[42]S/25354, op cit., paras. 57–58. See also, ibid., paras. 63, 91.

[43]Ibid., para. 101.

[44]*The United Nations and the Situation in the Former Yugoslavia*, DPI/1312/Rev. 2, March 1994, pp. 14–15. For a discussion of the creation of six "safe areas," namely, Srebrenica, Sarajevo, Tuzla, Zepa, Gorazde, and Bihac, see S/RES/819 (1993), April 16, 1993, and S/RES/824 (1993), May 6, 1993.

[45]Resolution 836 (1993) also decided that U.N. "Member States, acting nationally or through regional organizations or arrangements, may take . . . all necessary measures, through the use of air power, in and around safe areas . . . to support UNPROFOR in the performance of its mandate . . ." (para. 10). It is therefore inevitable to refer to Chapter VII in the resolution independently of the discussions in this part of the text.

[46]S/12611, March 19, 1978 (UNIFIL), para. 4(d). For other examples of guidelines with similar expressions, see, e.g., S/5653, April 11, 1964 (UNFICYP), para. 10; S/11052/Rev. 1, October 27, 1973 (UNEF-II), para. 4(d); S/12827, August 29, 1978 (UNTAG), para. 20; and Cf. S/24540, September 10, 1992 (UNPROFOR), para. 9.

[47]The guidelines for the U.N. force in Cyprus (UNFICYP) listed concrete examples in which the troops may be authorized to use force in self-defense. In addition to the defense of U.N. posts, premises, and vehicles under armed attack and the support of other personnel of UNFICYP under armed attack, the U.N. troops may be authorized to use force in such situations as (a) attempts by force to compel them to withdraw from a position that they occupy under orders from their commanders, or to infiltrate and envelop such positions as are deemed necessary by their commanders for them to hold, thus jeopardizing their safety; (b) attempts by force to disarm them; (c) attempts by force to prevent them from carrying out their responsibilities as ordered by their commanders; (d) violations by force of U.N. premises and attempts to arrest or abduct United Nations personnel, civil or military. S/5653, op. cit., paras. 16, 18. White even argues that the limitation to the use of force by peacekeepers in self-defense is "more akin to a personal right to self-defence by individual soldiers if shot at, rather than the much wider right of a State to self-defence." N.D. White, *Keeping the Peace: The United Nations and the Maintenance of International Peace and Security* (Manchester U.P., 1993), p. 204.

[48]Some members of the Council, in adopting Resolution 836 (1993), criticized its insufficiency and advocated that enforcement measures be taken to rebuff the Serb aggression. S/PV.3228, June 4, 1993, pp. 26 (Venezuela) and 27–30 (Pakistan).

[49]In any case, it should be noted that there was a qualitative difference between the tasks of UNOSOM-II under Resolution 814 (1993) and those of UNPROFOR under Resolution 836 (1993); the former being actively to disarm the local clan militias, while the latter passively to respond to the bombardments or deliberate obstructions by the local parties. Moreover, while UNOSOM-II actually conducted a use of force against those belonging to the Aidid faction several times, UNPROFOR in Bosnia does not seem to have resorted to the authorized use of force beyond self-defense so far.

[50]In the proposed mandate, the Secretary-General stated, amplifying the principle of self-defense, that the "basic element involved is clearly the prohibition against any *initiative* in the use of armed force" [emphasis in original]. See S/4389, July 18, 1960.

[51]See Oscar Schachter, "Authorized Uses of Force by the United Nations and Regional Organizations," in Damrosch and Scheffer (eds.), *Law and Force,* op cit., p. 85. As regards Resolution 161A, Dag Hammarskjöld, the then Secretary-General, considered that it stopped short of allowing U.N. troops to take the initiative in an armed attack on an organized army group and did not derogate from the position that U.N. troops should not become parties to armed conflict in the Congo. He also understood that the resolution, without any change of the U.N. mandate, widened its scope and application. S/4752, February 27, 1961, Annex VII, cited in Siekmann, *Basic Documents,* op cit., p. 110. On the other hand, Professor Bowett argues that "it is difficult to avoid the conclusion that the Security Council by this Resolution [161 A] abandoned a strict reliance on the principle of self-defence." D.W. Bowett, *United Nations Forces: A Legal Study* (Praeger, 1964), pp. 201–02.

[52]"Interview with Brian Urquhart," *Yomiuri Shinbun,* November 17, 1993; Brian Urquhart, *Ralph Bunche: An American Life* (W.W. Norton & Company, 1993), pp. 299–360, esp. pp. 329–330.

[53]Cf. Weiss, "New Challenges for UN Military Operations," op cit., p. 61.

[54]A/48/403–S/26450, op cit., para. 4(c).

[55]For an argument in this line at around the same period, see, e.g., John Mackinlay and Jarat Chopra, "Second Generation Multilateral Operations," *Washington Quarterly* 15:3 (Summer 1992), p. 120.

[56]See, e.g., *United Nations Peace-Keeping,* DPI/1399, August 1993; Boutros-Ghali, *Report on the Work of the Organization,* September 1993, op cit., pp. 175–76; *United Nations Peace-Keeping Operations,* op cit.; A/48/403–S/26450, op cit., para. 27.

[57]S/25859, May 28, 1993, p. 1; A/49/136, May 2, 1994, para. 40.

[58]Shigeru Kozai, "PKO Henshitsu-ron no Ayausa [The Danger of Arguing for 'the Transformed Peace-keeping Operations']," *Komei,* August 1994, pp. 22, 25. A.B. Fetherston, *Making United Nations Peacekeeping More Peaceful: Relating Concepts of 'Success' to Field Reality,* Working Paper No. 139 (Peace Research Centre, ANU, 1993), p. 21, lists, among others, UNIKOM, UNPROFOR in Bosnia-Herzegovina, and UNOSOM-II under the heading of "Are These Missions Peacekeeping?" China always expresses reservations on invoking Chapter VII in peacekeeping operations. See, e.g., S/PV.3174, op cit., p. 21; S/PV.3189, op cit., p. 16; S/PV.3228, op cit., p. 49; and S/PV.3286, October 4, 1993, p. 9.

[59]S/23280, op cit., Annex II, paras. 10–11, 13; S/23592, February 15, 1992, para. 22. Cf. S/24540, op cit., para. 9.

[60]S/25859, op cit., p. 1.

[61]UNIKOM, the other peacekeeping operation functioning under Chapter VII, does not fall under this category, because its use of force is limited to the case of self-defense. See *supra* note (33).

[62]Takahiro Shinyo, "Posuto-Reisenki no Kokuren-Heiwaiji-Katsudo no Shin-Ten-kai [New Developments in the United Nations Peace-Keeping Operations in the Post–Cold War Era]," *Handai Hogaku [Osaka Law Review]* 43:4 (March 1994), p. 7. See also S/PV.3114, September 14, 1992, p. 12 (China).

[63]Since Major General Mohammed Siad Barre fled Mogadishu in January 1991, there has been no effectively functioning government in Somalia. For a brief history of the Somali debacle, see Jeffrey Clark, "Debacle in Somalia," *Foreign Affairs* 72:1 (1992/93), pp. 110–12.

[64]*National Public Radio*, March 23, 1993 (available in LEXIS, News Library, Allnews File). See also James B. Steinberg, "International Involvement in the Yugoslavia Conflict," in Lori Fisler Damrosch (ed.), *Enforcing Restraint: Collective Intervention in Internal Conflicts* (Council on Foreign Relations Press, 1993), pp. 64–65. Difficulties have also been demonstrated in other parts of the former Yugoslavia where a civil war is being fought. In Croatia, the local Serbs came to feel betrayed and even to see UNPROFOR as a hostile presence, partly because of the latter's failure to protect them from the Croatian attack in January 1993, and partly because of the adoption by the Security Council of Resolution 815 of March 30, 1993, which explicitly stated, contrary to the perspective of local Serb people aspiring to sovereignty (the self-proclaimed Serb Republic of Krajina), that the UNPAs constitute "integral parts of the territory of the Republic of Croatia" (para. 5). Cf. S/25264, op cit., para. 16; S/25777, May 15, 1993, paras. 5–6. At the same time, the Croatian authority also continues to criticize the presence of UNPROFOR as preserving the fruits of the Serbs' illegal use of force. Steinberg, "International Involvement in the Yugoslavia Conflict," op cit., p. 63.

[65]In his "Summary Study," the Secretary-General stated in relation to the observer mission in Lebanon that "it is unlikely that a United Nations force could have operated without soon becoming a party to the internal conflicts." A/3943, op cit., para. 151.

[66]The task was transferred to UNPROFOR. Resolution 776 of September 14, 1992, authorized, "in implementation of paragraph 2 of resolution 770 (1992)," the enlargement of UNPROFOR's mandate and strength in Bosnia. Resolution 776 (1992) did not, however, vest UNPROFOR with enforcement power under Chapter VII. See *The United Nations and the Situation in the Former Yugoslavia*, DPI/1312/Rev. 2, op cit., pp. 5–6; S/PV.3114, op cit., pp. 4, 7–8, and 11–12.

[67]S/23445, January 20, 1992, Annex I and II; S/RES/733, January 23, 1992, pr. para. 1. The Somali delegate was present at the Security Council meeting during the deliberation of the resolution and did not express any objection to it. See S/PV.3039, January 23, 1992.

[68]*The United Nations and the Situation in Somalia*, United Nations Reference Paper, April 30, 1993, p. 1; John R. Bolton, "Wrong Turn in Somalia," *Foreign Affairs* 73:1 (January/February 1994), p. 57.

[69]S/25354, op cit., para. 91. Cf. S/24992, December 19, 1992, paras. 37–38.

[70]For Resolution 836 (1993), see *supra* note (45). NATO established a 20-kilometer exclusion zone, which may be subject to its air strikes, around Sarajevo on February 9, 1994, and similar zones around Gorazde and four other "safe areas" on April 22, 1994. *NATO Press Release*, (94)–15, February 9, 1994; (94)–31, April 22, 1994; (94)–32, April 22, 1994.

[71]*Yomiuri Shinbun*, April 14, 1994; *Reuters World Service*, September 27, 1994 (available in LEXIS News Library, Allnews File).

[72]S/RES/792 (1992), November 30, 1992, para. 10.

[73]Moreover, there was at that time no deployment of UNITAF or UNOSOM troops in the north and in border areas of Somalia, where security continued to be a matter of grave concern. The area under UNITAF control comprised only 40 percent of the territory. *The United Nations and the Situation in Somalia*, op cit., p. 8; S/25354, op cit., para. 6. The short-term deployment of UNITAF with a limited mission and its swift transition to a U.N. force had been pre-determined by the United States, which led the coalition forces. See Bolton, "Wrong Turn in Somalia," op cit., pp. 58–62.

[74]Henry Wiseman, "Peacekeeping in the International Political Context: Historical Analysis and Future Directions," in Rikhye and Skjelsbaek (eds.), *The United Nations and Peacekeeping,* op cit., p. 42.

[75]Professor Higgins argues that: "Everything about the situation in the former Yugoslavia has made it unsuitable for peacekeeping, and appropriate for enforcement action." Rosalyn Higgins, "The New United Nations and Former Yugoslavia," *International Affairs* (London) 69:3 (July 1993), p. 170.

[76]More than three quarters of post–Cold War peacekeeping operations have served in internal conflict situations. See also Alan James, "Internal Peace-keeping: A Dead End for the UN?," *Security Dialogue* 24:4 (December 1993), p. 358; Gene M. Lyons, "A New Collective Security: The United Nations and International Peace," *Washington Quarterly* 17:2 (Spring 1994), pp. 180–84.

[77]Goulding, "The Evolution of United Nations Peacekeeping," op cit., p. 451.

[78]Cf. A/48/403/Add. 1–S/26450/Add. 1, November 2, 1993, paras. 2–3 (Australia).

[79]Such an idea has long been considered in the United Nations and elsewhere. See, e.g., A/47/253, op cit., paras. 104–07. Recently, Secretary-General Boutros-Ghali proposed a transfer of peacekeeping operations from under the U.N. auspices to under those of the regional agencies, mainly for financial reasons. *Sankei Shinbun,* August 13, 1994.

[80]The British army is drawing lessons from UNOSOM-II and other operations as follows: If a peacekeeping force crosses the impartiality divide from peacekeeping to peace enforcement, and is thus perceived to be taking sides, the force loses its legitimacy and credibility as a trustworthy third party, thereby prejudicing its security. It will before long find itself among the parties to the conflict. To cross the impartiality divide is also to cross a Rubicon. On the other side of the impartiality divide, there is very little chance of getting back, and the only way out is likely to be by leaving the theatre. Mats R. Berdal, "Fateful Encounter: The United States and UN Peacekeeping," *Survival* 36:1 (Spring 1994), p. 44.

[81]S/RES/897 (1994), February 4, 1994. See also S/1994/12, January 6, 1994, paras. 55–57.

[82]S/RES/912 (1994), April 21, 1994, para. 8; S/1994/470, April 20, 1994, paras. 12–19. The Secretary-General's proposal came, as a means to secure a ceasefire in Rwanda, soon after the incident resulting in the deaths of the Presidents of Rwanda and Burundi.

[83]David Gompert, "How to Defeat Serbia," *Foreign Affairs* 73:4 (July/August 1994), pp. 38–39.

JOHN D.
ISAACS

# 2

AKIHIKO
TANAKA

# THE DOMESTIC CONTEXT:
## AMERICAN POLITICS, JAPANESE POLITICS, AND U.N. PEACEKEEPING

## JOHN D. ISAACS | THE DOMESTIC CONTEXT: AMERICAN POLITICS AND U.N. PEACEKEEPING

Since the advent of the Clinton Administration, there has been a disconnect between the public's consistent and strong support for U.N. peacekeeping and the irresolution and doubts in the U.S. Congress and Executive Branch. This disconnect will prove costly for future efforts in the United States to support the United Nations unless that general public support is translated into effective action.

Congressional views toward the United Nations today are being shaped particularly by the Organization's responses to world crises. The more effective the United Nations is in preventing and containing violence, the more favorably the United Nations will be viewed. Unfortunately, the reverse is true as well. Events in Bosnia may further jeopardize congressional support for the United Nations.

The disparity of opinion between the public and the government is one sign of the confusion in the United States as this country tries to develop a coherent foreign policy for the post–Cold War era. Congress has wavered between support for and opposition to a robust U.N. peacekeeping policy. The Clinton Administration has hesitated as well. Many Republicans who advocated an aggressive U.S. interventionist policy during the 1980s now wish to retreat militarily to our shores. Many Democrats, on the other hand, have switched from opposition to U.S. force projection abroad to championing multilateral intervention today.

The Bush Administration provided a powerful boost to the United Nations. President Bush developed a plan for paying back bills due to the United Nations, worked for a reformed and strengthened institution, took the unusual step of obtaining Security Council approval for Desert Storm, and operated in Somalia under the U.N. auspices—albeit with both military operations chiefly under American control. Congressional Democrats largely endorsed the Bush Administration policies.

The Clinton Administration then came into office inclined toward strong support for multilateral peacekeeping through the United Nations and regional organizations. Following a series of setbacks in Congress, however, the death of eighteen American soldiers in Somalia in October 1993, and the failed policy in Bosnia, the Administration began backtracking.

A draft Clinton peacekeeping policy languished for months over lack of a consistent strategy for dealing with congressional skepticism toward peace operations and due to inter-agency conflict between the State Department and the Department of Defense. The document that resulted from this policy review was published in May 1994. Presidential Decision Directive 25 (PDD-25) did not settle American policy but rather provided a benchmark from which U.S. policy will further evolve.

In the meantime, U.N. peacekeeping has become a polarized issue in Congress: For the past two years, most Democrats have supported the Administration's funding requests and new peacekeeping policy, while many Republicans have accused the President of allowing the United Nations to undermine American freedom of action. The enormous Republican electoral gains of November 1994 bode poorly for future U.S. support of U.N. peacekeeping.

## THE AMERICAN PUBLIC

Public support for the United Nations continues to be strong despite questions in Washington about the institution's effectiveness and the difficulties encountered in Somalia, Bosnia, and Rwanda.

In June 1994, the Americans Talk Issues Foundation conducted an in-depth survey of 1,000 individuals on the United Nations and global issues. The survey, as reported by Foundation President Alan F. Kay in a July 25, 1994, speech, found "enormous support for the U.N. by Americans . . . so broad and surprisingly deep that the story is *why don't we know the story.*" While Americans support an expansive role for the United Nations, they simultaneously question whether the United Nations has succeeded in its new missions.

Looking at one of the more controversial U.N. roles, the survey showed that 62 percent of Americans say that it is extremely important for the United Nations to do a better job of nation-building—"establishing a basic government, restoring basic services where the existing governments have collapsed"—while 28 percent say that this job is somewhat or not at all important. But only 27 percent rate the United Nations as doing an excellent or good job at these tasks, while 68 percent rate the job performance as poor or just fair. Similarly, 63 percent of Americans agree it is extremely important for the United Nations to organize a military force to enter a country that launches military action against a neighbor, but 54 percent feel that the United Nations is not performing this job well.

Additional evidence on support for the United Nations came from a four-nation poll released in April 1994 by *The New York Times*, *The Guardian* newspaper in Britain, *Der Spiegel* magazine in Germany, and the *Asahi Shimbun* newspaper in Japan. *The New York Times* reported on April 2 that "the poll revealed resounding support for the United Nations and for sending United Nations troops to enforce peace in the world's trouble spots."

By a margin of 77 to 21 percent, Americans said that the United Nations had contributed to world peace. An astounding 89 percent of Americans said it was important to cooperate with other countries by working through the United Nations. And whatever the American people's reluctance to commit U.S. troops to conflict overseas, the poll indicated that by a 59 to 31 percent margin, the United States "has a responsibility to contribute military troops to enforce peace plans in trouble spots around the world when it is asked by the United Nations."

These results followed a poll conducted March 4-8, 1994, for *The Wall Street Journal* and NBC by Republican and Democratic public opinion analysts. The survey, which compared public attitudes toward a variety of public figures and institutions, found that the United Nations engendered the most positive opinion in the group:

| Feelings Toward | Positive | Negative |
|---|---|---|
| United Nations | 48% | 21% |
| Bill Clinton | 47 | 33 |
| Hillary R. Clinton | 47 | 33 |
| Al Gore | 44 | 26 |
| NATO | 40 | 14 |
| Bob Dole | 36 | 28 |
| Oliver North | 30 | 38 |

What is particularly astonishing is that the level of support for the United Nations has remained elevated despite its noted problems. An earlier *Wall Street Journal* and NBC poll conducted in October 1993 asked the question:

> *When the United States is asked to be part of a United Nations international peacekeeping force in a troubled part of the world, should we take part or leave this job to other countries?*

Seventy-one percent of respondents said take part, 23 percent said leave the job to others, and 6 percent were not sure.

When ABC News asked in October 1993,

> *Generally speaking, do you think the United States should or should not send U.S. troops to participate in United Nations peacekeeping efforts around the world,*

58 percent said the United States should, 39 percent said the United States should not, and 3 percent had no opinion.

A Gallup/*USA Today* poll the same month posed the question:

> *Do you generally approve or disapprove of American troops participating in peacekeeping forces under the United Nations command?*

Fifty-eight percent approved, 37 percent disapproved, and 4 percent had no opinion.

All three polls were taken at the height of the controversy over U.S. policy in Somalia.

Historically, both *during and after* the Cold War, American public support for cooperation with the United Nations has remained consistently high. The *Los Angeles Times Mirror* and Potomac Associates have tracked public opinion for the last three decades. Over the years, these organizations have framed the question as follows:

> *Now I want to read you a list of statements. Please tell me whether you agree or disagree with each statement: ("No opinion" responses omitted.)*
>
> *A. The United States should cooperate fully with the United Nations.*
>
> *B. Since the United States is the most powerful nation in the world, we should go on our own way in international matters, not worrying too much about whether other countries agree with us or not.*

*C. We should not think so much in international terms but concentrate more on our own national problems and building up our strength and prosperity at home.*

| Date | A. Cooperate Fully with United Nations | | B. Go Our Own Way Internationally | | C. Concentrate On Domestic Problems | |
|------|-------|----------|-------|----------|-------|----------|
| | Agree | Disagree | Agree | Disagree | Agree | Disagree |
| | *Times Mirror* | | | | | |
| 10/93 | 64% | 28% | (not asked) | | (not asked) | |
| 4/93 | 71 | 22 | 34% | 63% | 18% | 79% |
| | *Potomac* | | | | | |
| 10/91 | 77 | 17 | 29 | 66 | 16 | 78 |
| 4/85 | 56 | 35 | 26 | 70 | 34 | 60 |
| 4/83 | 58 | 32 | 28 | 67 | 26 | 68 |
| 2/80 | 59 | 28 | 26 | 66 | 30 | 61 |
| 5/76 | 46 | 41 | 29 | 62 | 22 | 73 |
| 8/75 | 56 | 30 | 23 | 67 | 18 | 71 |
| 1/74 | 66 | 20 | 32 | 67 | 14 | 77 |
| 6/72 | 63 | 28 | 22 | 72 | 20 | 73 |
| 1968 | 72 | 21 | 23 | 72 | 31 | 60 |
| 1964 | 72 | 16 | 19 | 70 | 32 | 66 |

## CONGRESS

Congress has wavered in its attitude toward an expanded and more expensive U.N. peacekeeping policy. Congressional attitudes toward U.N. peace operations have been more sensitive than the public's to daily newspaper headlines, the shifting tides of politics, and the exigencies of the Congressional budget process. Senator Pete Domenici (R-NM) made the connection starkly during an April 21, 1994, Appropriations subcommittee hearing:

*I think in the United States Senate, at least, what's going on in Bosnia right now and what is the American policy and what chance we have for some success, if we know*

*what success is, I think that's all going to become part
of whether we can pay out arrearage for peacekeeping.*

Concerned over setbacks abroad, uncertain over post-Cold
War policy, focused on the U.N.'s failures rather than its successes,
and facing severe federal budget constraints, Congress has been
both more critical of U.N. peace operations than has the American
public and more determined to force changes in Administration
policies perceived as too sympathetic to the United Nations. This
prodding became especially conspicuous after Bill Clinton replaced
George Bush, freeing Republicans in Congress from the need to
support a Republican President.

Congress can shape U.S. policy toward the United Nations
in at least four ways:

1. It can use its power of the purse to cut funding for the U.S.
   share of the peacekeeping budget and thereby limit what
   the United States and the United Nations can accomplish;

2. It can place restrictions or conditions on funds to force
   modification of policies and practices, such as demanding
   that the United Nations establish an independent Inspector
   General's office;

3. It can set deadlines for troop withdrawals or limits on U.S.
   involvement in U.N. peace operations; and

4. It can seek to influence Administration policy toward specific U.N. operations through amendments, speeches,
   hearings, meetings, and letters.

Since the advent of the Clinton Administration, Congress has
wielded all four methods to influence U.S. policy toward the United
Nations. And it is the critics' voices and actions—claiming to speak
for the American public—that have been particularly loud and
effective in dampening Administration enthusiasm for a robust U.N.
peacekeeping policy.

U.N. supporters in Congress have often been drowned out by
the critics. In part, that is because some of the U.N.'s chief antagonists have been in key positions—and will be even more so in the
next two years—overseeing funding for U.N. peacekeeping. In the
Senate, two of the U.N.'s most persistent critics—Robert Byrd
(D-WV) and Ernest Hollings (R-SC)—have controlled the flow of
peacekeeping funds as chairman of the full Appropriations Commit-

tee and head of the subcommittee that handles the bulk of the funding.

Byrd in particular has not been shy about advancing his views. In a July 1, 1993, speech on the Senate floor, Byrd said that U.N. activities look "suspiciously as though the United States is still trying to play the role of the world's policeman—a supercop covered by a United Nations multilateral cloak." He continued: "Neither the United States nor the United Nations is, or can be, the white knight that rides to the rescue of every damsel in distress." Two weeks later, Byrd said: "I do not believe that the American people are eager to spend their hard-earned tax dollars on a series of global U.N. enforcement actions which have, at best, a rather murky goal and a limited chance of success."

Byrd is in an important position to ensure that his words are followed up by deeds: In February 1994, he virtually single-handedly knocked out the Administration's request to pay $670 million in arrearages for U.N. peacekeeping. In the fall of 1993, amendments he offered forced the President to set a date for the withdrawal of U.S. soldiers from Somalia.

Ironically, despite their criticisms, Hollings and Byrd cooperated to secure substantial peacekeeping funding in 1994. Both helped to restore the $670 million in another bill later in the year and to fund the Administration's full peacekeeping request in fiscal 1995.

House committee leadership also made a difference on peacekeeping decisions. In 1993, two skeptics on peacekeeping—Neal Smith (D-IA) and Harold Rogers (R-KY)—used their leadership positions on a key Appropriations subcommittee to chop back Administration requests for peacekeeping funding. By fortuitous chance, in mid-1994, David Obey (D-WI) took over leadership of the House Appropriations Committee, and Alan Mollohan (D-WV), a peacekeeping supporter, became chairman of the Commerce, Justice, State, and Judiciary Subcommittee. The impact of the Republican Congressional victory on peacekeeping was mixed. Although Rogers replaced Mollohan as chairman of the key House Appropriations subcommittee, in the Senate, a U.N. supporter, Mark Hatfield (R-OR), became chairman of the Appropriations Committee.

Congress deals with U.N. issues primarily through the prism of funding; the Administration's U.N. authorization and appropriation requests have become the primary venue for amendments to cut peacekeeping funding or place restrictions on Administration policy. The fights have grown increasingly fierce as the rising costs of peacekeeping collide with many other Administration and congressional priorities, and funding restrictions can be used to limit U.S. involvement in the United Nations. In fiscal 1989, the U.S. share of U.N. peacekeeping totaled $29 million; by fiscal 1991 it had increased to $107 million. In fiscal 1994, the amount reached $670 million, but it dropped to $533 million in fiscal 1995, and the House Appropriations Committee cut the figure for fiscal 1996 further to $425 million.

## MAJOR U.N. ISSUES DEBATED IN CONGRESS

**Costs and budgetary priorities.** U.N. proponents argue that a billion dollars is minuscule compared with military spending; a country that can afford $263 billion annually for the Pentagon can easily afford to keep up with its international obligations. Yet that billion dollars competes directly in the congressional budget process with money for crime programs in the Justice Department, economic stimulus projects in the Commerce Department, the FBI, the State Department, the Civil Rights Commission, the Securities and Exchange Commission, and many more programs. Since the Reagan revolution and skyrocketing federal budget deficits, money has been tight for any expanded program, domestic or foreign. An additional dollar for peacekeeping within the Commerce, Justice, State, and Judiciary Subcommittee is a dollar that is not available for another program. Senator Domenici hammered this point home on April 21, 1994:

> I just want to put in perspective that the president's entire new crime initiative will cost less than what it will cost for 25,000 troops if we ever put them in Bosnia.

**Jurisdictional confusion.** The funding problem in Congress is compounded by the fact that U.N. and peacekeeping funding decisions are spread among 14 subcommittees and committees. For example, one appropriations subcommittee is asked to fund most peacekeeping operations, a second approves "voluntary" peacekeeping contributions, and a third has to consider the Pentagon's share.

**Size of U.S. peacekeeping assessment.** These financial problems are exacerbated by the large share of peacekeeping costs that the United States currently pays—over 30 percent. Critics of the increasing costs for the United States can use as one debating point the high portion the United States is forced to pay compared with other wealthy countries.

**U.S. military involvement abroad.** Another problem is that the United Nations has become a fulcrum for the larger debate over U.S. involvement abroad. Many of the most conservative hawks who had for years favored the aggressive containment of communism now wish to retreat militarily to our shores. They believe that problems in Somalia or Rwanda, however horrific, simply do not impinge on our vital interests. They further object to sending U.S. troops or to paying for dealing with these problems. These conservatives are joined by some liberals who advocate spending money to cure problems at home, such as housing shortages, unaffordable health care, unemployment, and education deficiencies, before spending on conflicts overseas.

These two groups united in a pivotal Senate debate in October 1993 over whether to pull U.S. troops out of the U.N. peacekeeping operation in Somalia. While President Clinton and the Democratic leadership managed to stave off this maneuver, the President was forced to agree to a six-month timetable for withdrawal. That Senate debate was followed immediately by one over whether to place U.S. troops under foreign command. Many in Congress cringe at the thought of U.S. forces commanded by U.N. military leaders—notwithstanding the fact that U.S. troops have served under foreign generals in many past conflicts, from the Revolutionary War to the Persian Gulf War.

**U.N. management.** Another refrain heard in Congress is that the United Nations is badly managed. Senator Larry Pressler (R-SD), for example, argued for limitations upon U.N. funding until an independent Inspector General's office could be established to review the U.N.'s books. Pressler claimed that the United Nations has proved incapable of managing its financial affairs, and so it cannot be expected to have the oversight capacity to run peacekeeping operations around the world. "Time and time again, I have raised the issue of U.N. budgetary waste, fraud, and abuse," said Pressler on July 28, 1993. "Repeatedly, though, my pleas for strong corrective mechanisms have fallen on deaf ears."

**U.N. command structure for the military.** The critique of the U.N.'s administrative ability is intensified when the discussion turns to the Organization's ability to handle military operations. Many in Congress argue that the United Nations does not have either the expertise or the infrastructure to enable it to manage effectively peace operations. Nor, they add, does the United Nations have military commanders capable of handling the tasks involved in peacekeeping operations. However, the United States and other countries have largely ignored U.N. Secretary-General Boutros Boutros-Ghali's proposals for a strengthened military capacity.

**U.S. foreign policy subcontracted to the United Nations.** Then there is the claim that President Clinton has "subcontracted" major portions of U.S. foreign policy to the United Nations. Members of Congress have expressed concern that the United Nations will get the United States involved in operations that do not involve U.S. national interests. There is an additional concern that the United Nations will become a powerful institution that can override American national interests. Then Speaker-to-be Newt Gingrich, in an Ohio speech on April 19, 1994, stated, "To me, it is profoundly wrong to be substituting the United Nations for the United States."

**Peacekeeping detracts from military readiness.** Finally, there is a concern that any Pentagon contribution for U.N. peacekeeping detracts from the military's mission of fighting and winning wars. Pentagon defenders argue that the more U.S. forces participate in U.N. peace operations, the more the readiness of the American military will decline, undermining its ability to fight simultaneously two regional wars.

## IMPACT OF CONGRESSIONAL CRITICISM

Congressional criticisms of the United Nations have taken their toll. In 1993, Congress rejected the Administration's request for $293 million for a back-payment on peacekeeping, and it cut one-third of the new request for peacekeeping contributions of $620 million. It also refused to accept a separate Pentagon account proposed by the Administration to pay for future U.S. involvement in peacekeeping operations.

In April 1994, when Congress approved the State Department conference report authorizing funding for peacekeeping, it tacked on:

1. A provision withholding 50 percent of the $670 million for peacekeeping arrearages plus a portion of the U.S. contribution to the U.N. budget until the United Nations creates a permanent Inspector General office;

2. A ceiling on U.S. contributions for U.N. peacekeeping to no more than 30.4 percent of total U.N. peacekeeping costs in fiscal 1995 and to 25 percent in fiscal 1996; and

3. A requirement for the President to notify Congress 15 days prior to providing American funds for peacekeeping missions.

After the release of the Administration's peacekeeping policy in May 1994, and following Mollohan's installation as chairman of a key Appropriations subcommittee, the outlook for U.N. funding improved significantly. Congress, taking a second look at the proposition, reversed itself and approved the full supplemental appropriations request of $670 million in fiscal 1994 plus the $533 million requested in fiscal 1995.

In addition, with the Executive Branch and House leadership better organized, the House three times in 1994 defeated Republican amendments aimed at cutting peacekeeping funding:

1. On May 24, 1994, the House defeated, by a vote of 221 to 191, an amendment offered by Floyd Spence (R-SC) to limit peacekeeping funding;

2. On June 27, 1994, the House defeated a Rogers amendment (228-178) that would have cut peacekeeping costs and transferred $207 million to the states for hiring police and incarcerating illegal aliens; and

3. On August 10, 1994, the House defeated another Rogers amendment to accept Senate cuts in peacekeeping (250-177).

Similarly, by a healthy 61-35 vote, Armed Services Committee chairman Sam Nunn (R-GA), with help from Carl Levin (D-MI) and Jim Jeffords (R-VT), managed to turn back an attempt to eliminate peacekeeping funding in the Pentagon money bill.

These successes were also accompanied by setbacks. Ultimately, Congress rejected the Administration plan to have the Pentagon share responsibility with the Department of State for peacekeeping funding. Moreover, U.N. funding measures proved susceptible in the Senate to politically hot-button amendments that transferred peacekeeping funding to states to pay for the incarceration of illegal aliens.

Republican control of Congress in 1995 further clouds the prospect for peacekeeping. The Republican "Contract with

America," which was signed by most Republican House candidates, focuses primarily on domestic issues, particularly cuts in taxes and government. U.N. peacekeeping, however, is but one of two specific targets within a skimpy national security platform that could lead to change. Republicans vow never to permit U.S. troops to be placed under foreign command, particularly as part of a U.N. peacekeeping force.

Republicans have pledged to cut government spending—exempting the Defense Department budget—while also cutting taxes. This pledge jeopardizes funding for hundreds of programs, including peacekeeping. The futility of U.N. efforts in Bosnia further undermines the credibility of all U.N. peace operations and fuels congressional criticism.

Moreover, Jesse Helms (R-NC), chair of the Senate Foreign Relations Committee, has placed U.N. peacekeeping on his target list for cuts. The new House Appropriations subcommittee chairman, Harold Rogers, as was previously noted, was already on the warpath in 1994.

## THE CLINTON ADMINISTRATION

Determined leadership by the Clinton Administration is critical to improving the U.N.'s standing in Congress. That leadership was a long time in coming, and it is still racked by some indecision and confusion. The President will be further tested with the Republicans in control of Congress.

The Administration came into office in 1993 determined to pursue what some officials labeled "aggressive multilateralism." During the campaign, Clinton had called for a U.N. "rapid deployment force. . .standing guard at the borders of countries threatened by aggression, preventing mass violence against civilian populations, providing relief and combating terrorism."

From the start, Madeleine Albright, U.S. Ambassador to the United Nations, was the consistent, if frequently lone, voice for a stronger U.N. role in solving the world's crises. She called for the United Nations to help rebuild the nation in civil war–torn Somalia. After the October 1993 American deaths in Somalia and controversy over policy in Bosnia, the Administration backed away from her assertive view of American policy. Running scared after widespread complaints from Congress, the Administration stalled its policy review for months. As reported in The Washington Post of April 24, 1994,

*The fallout from Somalia also sank a scheme to involve the United States heavily in peacekeeping. A watered-down policy for presentation to Congress, with heavy limits on U.S. participation, still awaits Clinton's signature after months of debate and revision.*

Administration officials and many in Europe began to use the United Nations as a scapegoat for their own policy failures. In Bosnia and Somalia, the Americans and Europeans gave the United Nations an expansive mandate to solve problems—but without providing the resources, guidance, or political backing to fulfill the job.

The Administration finally completed its U.N. policy review by May 1994, much later than the summer of 1993 date projected. That painfully slow decision-making reflected a wider Executive Branch difficulty in formulating a coherent foreign policy in an Administration primarily focused on domestic policy. The Administration's wavering policy toward the United Nations was paralleled by its vacillations over Bosnia, China, Haiti, and North Korea, and conventional arms sale policy.

A major part of the delay was that the National Security Council found it difficult to drive the bureaucracy toward decisions. That process was complicated by the inevitable inter-agency fighting, particularly between the Departments of State and Defense. The State Department wanted the Pentagon to pick up peacekeeping bills—as long as State could keep control over policy. The Pentagon was not about to pay more of the bills without more of the decision-making power. In 1993, this turf battle led to the State Department fighting against the establishment of a separate Pentagon peacekeeping account.

The upshot of the delay and rising criticism of Administration policy is that PDD-25 accentuated restrictions, caveats, and checklists that will inhibit U.S. involvement in U.N. peace operations instead of providing the basis for expanded multilateral peacekeeping. The Administration determined that it needed to re-establish credibility with Congress by stressing that it will not let the United Nations lead the United States into foreign entanglements that the United States does not embrace, and that U.S. troops will rarely be employed in U.N. operations.

In a February 6, 1994, *New York Times* article, National Security Adviser Anthony Lake assured Americans that "peacekeeping is not at the center of our foreign or defense policy." In the future, Lake said, the United States will be more "selective" in approving peace operations. "We are asking tough questions before voting for a peace operation at the U.N." He dismissed as unrealistic fears that "the Administration would subcontract its foreign policy to any power or person."

According to the new policy, in future crises the United States will ask if there is an identifiable endpoint to a U.N. peace operation, whether financial and military resources are available, whether domestic and congressional support can be marshalled, and many more questions. Answers must be supplied, not only before U.S. troops are committed, but before the United States will approve a U.N. operation even without a request for U.S. troops.

The policy also accentuated the U.S. drive to reduce U.N. peacekeeping costs, to reform U.N. administrative and military procedures, and to improve the U.N.'s military capacity. In addition, the policy tried to reassure Congress that the President will always retain command authority aver U.S. forces participating in U.N. peace operations. The document underscored that the United States will oppose a U.N. standing army or the earmarking of U.S. forces to serve in future peace operations.

PDD-25 was not without its positive aspects. It finally provided a basis for Administration unity on future peacekeeping policy. It divided funding and authority between State and Defense (although, as was previously noted, Congress still resists such a division). It committed the government to seek full funding for U.S. arrearages. It enshrined procedures for building congressional and public support for U.N. peace operations. And at a minimum, it ended months of indecision that had paralyzed American policy.

PDD-25 produced mixed results. On the one hand, Administration officials worked as a team to convince Congress to include full funding of arrearages, a process that proved remarkably successful in 1994. In addition, establishing a clear policy position may have helped to ease the concerns of some members of Congress over Administration indecisiveness on peacekeeping. On the other hand, in the first post–PDD-25 crisis, the slaughter in Rwanda, the Administration was very slow to react, holding up U.N. action for many months and leading international relief efforts only after the worst of the killings had ceased.

## CONCLUSION

In future years, American supporters of the United Nations will face a difficult challenge. U.N. dues and funds for peacekeeping are likely to be under siege. In 1996 the Clinton Administration's U.N. policy will be challenged by many in Congress. The Administration's likely response is not yet discernible. Administration policy on peacekeeping as on many other issues will depend on the overall relationship between the White House and the new Republican majority in Congress.

In recognition of the new policy terrain, it is likely that the Clinton Administration will proceed cautiously on U.N. issues. As the Administration's post–PDD-25 policy on Rwanda has already indicated, it will likely analyze the attitudes of the public and Congress and gauge the risks and costs to the United States before approving new U.N. peace operations or U.S. military involvement. More than likely, the Administration will go into a defensive crouch to defend requested U.N. funding levels.

U.N. supporters will have to organize. If the U.N. defenders focus too narrowly on reforming and strengthening the United Nations in its fiftieth year, they may be working to reform an institution that has been severely undercut by a series of small and large cuts delivered by Congress over the next two years. Attempts to strengthen an institution that is perceived to have failed in Bosnia and Rwanda may prove unavailing. If the United States, the world's remaining superpower, becomes unenthusiastic about supporting the United Nations, then the Organization's effectiveness will be severely undermined.

U.N. supporters would have to take a number of steps to influence both Congress and the President:

1. Develop a more persuasive national security case for the United Nations, one that convinces skeptics of the value of the United Nations in protecting U.S. interests.

2. Re-establish bi-partisan support for the institution, drawing on former Republican government officials and experts.

3. Build a strong coalition of U.N. supporters, including civic organizations, foreign policy specialists, religious groups, foreign aid groups, scientific organizations, labor unions, business groups, and others.

4. Work to translate the general public support for the United Nations into specific grassroots efforts to influence the President and Congress.

5. Promote U.N. reforms that may assist in building congressional support, including lowering the U.S. share of peacekeeping assessments and establishing the office of an independent Inspector General.

Events during 1993 had a disastrous impact on the U.N.'s position within the U.S. Congress and Executive Branch. As support waned in Congress, the Administration retreated in confusion, and peacekeeping funding suffered. Fortunately, the disasters of 1993 were not repeated in 1994. But developments in Bosnia have rekindled opposition to U.N. peacekeeping.

Powerful arguments can be advanced by the Administration and U.N. supporters in favor of U.N. peacekeeping. Crippling setbacks in Congress can be averted, but it will take determined Presidential leadership and effective public support to ensure that the Administration and Congress work for an effective United Nations capable of meeting the world's challenges.

## AKIHIKO TANAKA | THE DOMESTIC CONTEXT: JAPANESE POLITICS AND U.N. PEACEKEEPING

## BEFORE THE GULF WAR

The Japanese have long held a very favorable view of the United Nations. After the defeat in the Second World War, one of the most important goals of the Japanese was to be re-accepted by the international community. The symbolic goal of such re-entry into the international community was to become a member of the United Nations. Therefore, when Japan was accepted as a U.N. member in 1956, many Japanese felt that their nation had finally become a full-fledged member of the international community. The *Diplomatic Bluebook* published in the following year, the first edition of this annual publication, posited a "UN centered diplomacy" as one of the three pillars of Japanese diplomacy, with the other pillars being "diplomacy as an Asian nation" and "diplomacy as a nation in the liberal camp." The postwar sentiment of pacifism reinforced a rosy picture of the United Nations as a symbol of "peace."

But the Cold War environment did not allow Japan to pursue a "UN centered diplomacy" very much. Within a few years, the *Diplomatic Bluebook* ceased to use the concept of the "three pillars." A content analysis of the policy speeches of the postwar prime ministers reveals that reference to the United Nations was infrequent from the mid-1960s to the late 1980s with the exception of the early 1970s when reference to the United Nations was made with respect to China's admittance to the United Nations in 1971.[1]

The concept of U.N. peacekeeping was virtually unknown among the Japanese public for most of the postwar period. It is true that before Japan became a U.N. member, debates were conducted in the Diet as to the constitutionality of Japan's possible participation in a U.N. force when Japan became a U.N. member. But the debates were highly abstract and hypothetical. With its Constitution, which pledges to "renounce war as a sovereign right of the nation and the threat or use of force as a means of settling international disputes" and which prohibits the possession of "land, sea, and air forces, as well as other war potential," could Japan assume the responsibilities of a U.N. member under the U.N. Charter? This was the question then raised. The government answered that Article 43 of the Charter could be interpreted to suggest various possible ways of contributing to U.N. activities, the exact nature of which would be determined by "a special agreement or agreements" to be concluded between the member state and the Security Council. Thus, Japan's Constitution would not necessarily be an obstacle to Japanese membership in the United Nations. Japan's application for U.N. membership accordingly included a statement that Japan would fulfill all the obligations of a U.N. member "by all means at its disposal." Since no such "special agreements" have been made in the entire history of the United Nations, this question was a highly hypothetical and theoretical one.[2] In any case, the general atmosphere of Japanese politics did not allow any real possibility of sending Japanese troops abroad for whatever reason; the House of Councilors passed a resolution on June 22, 1954, to confirm its will not to allow dispatch of the Self-Defense Forces (SDF) abroad.[3]

Debate concerning the possibility of Japan participating in U.N. peacekeeping started as early as the 1960s. One stimulus for such debate was a request by then U.N. Secretary-General Dag Hammarskjöld that the Japanese government send officers of the SDF to participate in the U.N. Observer Group in Lebanon in July 1958. The Japanese government turned his request down on the argument that the mission might violate existing laws, if not the Constitution. In early 1961, the statement by Japan's then Ambassador to the United Nations aroused a controversy; Ambassador Koto Matsudaira was reported to have stated that he was in trouble when Japan refused Mr. Hammarskjöld's request and that "it is not consistent for Japan to adhere to UN cooperation on the one hand and to refuse all participation in the UN armies." The opposition parties demanded Ambassador Matsudaira's resignation. In the end, Mr. Matsudaira withdrew his statement.[4]

In response to criticisms by the opposition parties, the Director General of the Cabinet Legislation Bureau, Shuzo Hayashi, summarized the position of the government in the Diet in 1961. He said: "If the UN police activities are conducted in an ideal form, in other words, when a country that disrupted order within the UN system is to be punished, or in the case of establishing a police corps to maintain order, and if a unitary force under the United Nations is created with the participation of personnel dispatched by member countries, then [Japan's participation in such a force] would not be an act of a sovereign nation. Also there is a possibility of a peaceful police force which does not conduct military activities. These possibilities would not pose problems relating to the First Clause of Article 9."[5]

Sporadic mention of a "UN army" has been made on and off since then. It was in 1980 that the government announced another interpretation. It said: "It is impossible to discuss the right or wrong of Japan's participation in a UN force in general because the so-called UN forces have different objectives and missions. If the objectives and missions of the UN force in question include the use of force, we believe that the constitution does not allow the participation of the SDF in it. On the other hand, if their objectives and missions do not include the use of force, the constitution does not prohibit the participation of the SDF. But because the current SDF law does not give such a mission to the SDF, the SDF is not allowed to participate in it."[6]

But these legal debates were then considered very hypothetical. The media paid little attention when a group of specialists in international law and international politics urged the Japanese government, in 1983, to consider the possibility of participating in U.N. peacekeeping operations that did not involve the use of force.[7] By the late 1980s, however, the Ministry of Foreign Affairs made some noteworthy attempts to pave the way for Japan's participation in U.N. peacekeeping activities. In May 1988, the government of Prime Minister Noboru Takeshita proposed his "three pillars of international cooperation" concept, consisting of 1) cooperation for peace, 2) promotion of international cultural exchange, and 3) increase in official development assistance (ODA). According to Takeshita, "cooperation for peace" included "positive participation in diplomatic efforts, the dispatch of necessary personnel and the provision of financial cooperation, aiming at the resolution of regional conflicts."[8] In 1988, Japan sent one civilian to the U.N. Good Offices Mission in Afghanistan and Pakistan and another civilian to the U.N. monitoring operations on the Iran-Iraq truce (the U.N. Iran-Iraq Military Observer Group). In the following years, Japan assigned thirty-one civilian observers to the election monitoring team in Namibia (the U.N. Transition Assistance Group) and six civilian observers to join in monitoring the Nicaraguan elections. Nevertheless, by the end of the 1980s, no serious debates had taken place as to the possibility, let alone the desirability, of sending the SDF on U.N. missions.[9]

## THE GULF WAR

The Gulf War was the turning point in this debate. During the period from August 1990 to February 1991, Japan appeared totally unprepared to make timely and meaningful responses to this first international crisis of the post–Cold War era. Not only the government but also the general public seemed unprepared to make up their minds swiftly; pros and cons of various measures were voiced while Prime Minister Toshiki Kaifu vacillated in the middle. Many pundits demanded that the government do something, but they did not agree on what that something was. In the end, the lowest common denominator prevailed: a financial contribution plus some civilian activities. But the debate about Japan's contribution to U.N. peace activities was activated during and after the war. More than all Japan's postwar prime ministers, Toshiki Kaifu and Kiichi Miyazawa used the term "United Nations" most frequently in their policy speeches before the Diet.[10]

The first round of debate on Japan's relations with U.N. peace activities was centered on a "United Nations Peace Cooperation Bill" that the Kaifu government presented to the Diet in October 1990. However, this bill, sponsored mainly by the Ministry of Foreign Affairs, was doomed to failure. The bill provided for a U.N. Peace Cooperation Corps to cooperate with peacekeeping and other activities either based on U.N. resolutions or conducted to make U.N. resolutions effective. The Corps, in the bill, was to be composed of volunteers—personnel on loan from other government agencies, including the Maritime Safety Agency and the SDF. The tasks of the Corps were to include 1) monitoring of a truce, 2) providing administrative advice and guidance to the government after the conflict, 3) monitoring and managing elections, 4) providing transport and communication, 5) engaging in medical activities, 6) participating in refugee rescue operations, and 7) joining reconstruction activities. The Corps would not be allowed to engage in any "use of force" or "threat of use of force"; the members of the Corps were to carry only small weapons to be used for self-protection.

The bill did not pass even the House of Representatives, in which the ruling Liberal Democratic Party (LDP) had a majority, because the opposition parties, which controlled the House of Councilors, had made clear that they would not cooperate with the bill. The LDP leadership decided it was of no use to push the bill to a vote even in the lower house; there was even a prospect that some LDP members might abstain from voting, which would have embarrassed the leadership.

Several reasons for the failure of the bill may be pointed out. They include the vacillation of Prime Minister Kaifu, the clumsy responses on the part of the government in the Diet deliberations, and the failure of the LDP to persuade the second largest party— the Komeito, which had the swing votes in the upper house—to agree to the bill. But more importantly, the Japanese public did not support the bill. Various public opinion polls conducted in the autumn indicated that only 20 to 30 percent of the Japanese supported the bill.

In exchange for abandonment of the bill, the LDP leadership struck a deal with the Komeito and the Democratic Socialist Party (DSP) to the effect that it would cooperate in the future to create an organization, separate from the SDF, that could participate in U.N.–related activities, thus leaving open the possibility of Japan's more active participation in future U.N. peacekeeping operations. After the multinational forces started military action in January 1991, the Japanese government decided to send SDF aircraft for refugee transfers and to contribute $9 billion to the multinational forces. The former action did not materialize, however; no countries in the region or international organizations ever asked Japan to send planes. Therefore, virtually the only contribution that Japan made during the Gulf War was a massive financial one: $13 billion in total, which was raised by a tax increase.

## COLLECTIVE SECURITY AND JAPAN

One issue that was highlighted in the debate during the Gulf War was the relationship between the concept of "collective security" and the Japanese Constitution. Ichiro Ozawa, the LDP Secretary General, argued:

> With the end of the East-West Cold War, the concept of "collective security" centered on the United Nations is being utilized. The "collective security" based on the UN Charter is supposed to protect the global order. Its

*character is different from the use of the concept of "collective self-defense" that the government has considered unconstitutional. I believe the ideals of our constitution and the UN charter are identical. In order to preserve the constitutional principles of non-use of force and renunciation of war, we need to supplement (our defense efforts) with the collective security system centered on the United Nations.*[11]

Ozawa in essence argued that Japan could cooperate with U.N. activities, including military action, without changing the Constitution.

The government's official interpretation revealed by the Cabinet Legislation Council maintained the 1980 interpretation quoted above: Whether or not Japan could participate in a U.N. force depends on the nature of the force; if its mission includes the use of force, Japan could not participate in it. If a special agreement or agreements under Article 43 of the U.N. Charter is to be created, Japan has to decide what kind of agreement is allowed under the Constitution.[12]

There seem to be two fundamental differences between the view represented by Ozawa and the view stated at that time by the Cabinet Legislation Council. The first is the relationship between the concept of "collective security" and the "international disputes" mentioned in Article 9 of the Japanese Constitution. To quote Article 9 again, it says: "Aspiring sincerely to an international peace based on justice and order, the Japanese people forever renounce war as a sovereign right of the nation and the threat or use of force as means of settling international disputes." If the "international disputes" used here include "international disputes" between countries acting under the principle of "collective security" and a country or countries regarded as aggressors, Japan could not participate in such activities if they involve "the threat or use of force." On the other hand, as Ozawa argued, if the "international disputes" here mentioned are only those "international disputes" between sovereign nations without mediation by the system of collective security, then participation in the collective security system, even if it entails the "use of force" does not violate Article 9.

The second difference resides in the judgment over whether the current United Nations deserves the name of a true "collective security" system. Ozawa seemed to believe that virtually all actions conducted under the auspices of U.N. Security Council resolutions are based on Chapter VII. On the other hand, the Cabinet Legislation Council position was based on the belief that only a U.N. force in an ideal international community deserves the name of "collective security." Asked to compare his statements with those of his predecessors, the Director General of the Council responded that what they referred to was a "UN force" under an "ideal international society. . .one step beyond Chapter VII of the UN Charter." How Japan might participate in a U.N. force organized under Chapter VII, it was argued—considering the absence of this "ideal international society"—should depend upon whether or not the mission included the use of force.[13]

This debate did not proceed further. The LDP established a committee headed by Ozawa to examine the issue. The Ozawa committee drafted a report arguing for the adoption of the concept of "international security" (*kokusai-teki anzen hosho*) to allow Japan's participation in multinational forces and U.N. forces under U.N. resolutions. In essence, the report simply used the term "international security" instead of "collective security" to mean the same thing. But because the focus of the national debate after the Gulf War shifted from participation in multinational forces to participation in peacekeeping activities such as the one to be started in Cambodia, the issue of the relationship of "collective security" and Japan's Constitution was put on a back burner.

## THE PEACEKEEPING OPERATIONS BILL AND CAMBODIA

The second round of the Japanese debate on relations with U.N. peace activities started with the preparation of a new bill that would permit Japanese participation in U.N. peacekeeping operations (PKO). The debate began where the ill-fated U.N. Peace Cooperation Bill ended: with the three-party agreement among the LDP, Komeito, and the DSP. As was stated above, the three-party arrangement indicated that a new organization other than the SDF would be created to assume the role of sending personnel to U.N. peacekeeping missions. The Socialist Party, which was adamantly opposed to any dispatch of SDF personnel to the Gulf War for whatever purposes, was not in opposition to U.N. peacekeeping operations *per se*. Therefore, the Socialist Party also proposed a plan to create a "Peace Cooperation Corps" composed totally of civilians. Some signs of convergence in views seemed to emerge in the spring of 1991.

But in the summer, after three groups of Diet members from the LDP, the Japan Socialist Party (JSP), Komeito, and the DSP returned from their observation of actual U.N. peacekeeping operations abroad, the LDP, Komeito, and the DSP shifted away from their original agreement. They began to argue that the participation of militarily trained personnel was essential to carry out the task of U.N. peacekeeping and that the best way to accomplish this would be to utilize the SDF personnel by double-appointing them to a new organization to carry out peacekeeping. However, the Socialists could not accept the participation of the SDF.

Now the task for the three parties was to create the conditions under which they could justify the dispatch of the SDF for peacekeeping without being condemned for violating the Constitution. If all of them and the majority of the Japanese public had accepted Ozawa's arguments, they would not have had to worry about conditions. But the fact is that neither Komeito nor the DSP would accept Ozawa's viewpoints on "collective security." They wanted to determine the types of peacekeeping activities that were consistent with the interpretation of the Constitution advocated by the government until then. Thus the "Five PKO Principles" were created in late July 1991:

1. Agreement on a ceasefire shall have been reached among the parties in the conflict.
2. The parties in the conflict, including the territorial state(s), shall have given their consent to deployment of the peacekeeping forces and Japan's participation in the force.
3. The peacekeeping force shall strictly maintain impartiality, not favoring any party in the conflict.
4. Should any of the above guideline requirements cease to be satisfied, the government of Japan may withdraw its contingent.
5. Use of weapons shall be limited to the minimum necessary to protect the lives of personnel.[14]

The Kaifu government, based on the above understanding, presented a new bill, which was often called the "PKO bill," in September 1991. The passage of the bill was difficult. Even among the three parties, there were several points of contention. The DSP insisted that prior Diet approval was essential to the participation of Japanese personnel in U.N. operations. Among the followers of Komeito there appeared strong voices of dissent with respect to the SDF's involvement in the peacekeeping force. In the meantime, Prime Minister Toshiki Kaifu, unable to push his political reform bills through the Diet, resigned and was replaced by Kiichi Miyazawa in November 1991.

In order to break the deadlock, Komeito proposed in the spring of 1992 to "freeze" the so-called "core" missions of peacekeeping forces—monitoring disarmament, patrolling ceasefire zones, inspecting the disposal of abandoned weapons—until such time as a new separate law would "unfreeze" these missions (see Appendix). The LDP and the DSP agreed with Komeito on the "freeze," and the LDP and Komeito agreed with the DSP as to the need for Diet approval. The Socialists, however, would not accept such a deal and in many ways became more rigid than in the previous year; they repeated all kinds of filibuster techniques, such as *gyuho* (ox-walk), but they could not stop passage of peacekeeping legislation. The bill was approved by the Diet in June 1992, thus enabling for the first time since the end of World War II the dispatch of the SDF for U.N. peacekeeping missions abroad. But because of the compromise of freezing the "core" of peacekeeping missions, the activities that the SDF can conduct under the law are limited to logistical support, which includes medical care, transportation, and construction.

Under the PKO law, now officially called the "International Peace Cooperation Law," Japan sent, in September 1992, approximately 600 SDF construction unit personnel, eight military observers, 75 civilian police monitors, and 41 civilian election monitors to the U.N. Transitional Authority in Cambodia (UNTAC) operations. The UNTAC successfully conducted the first national election in Cambodia in May 1993 and concluded its mission in September 1993. During the UNTAC operations, about 60 personnel lost their lives, including two Japanese: a civilian police officer and a U.N. volunteer.

Japanese forces were also sent to Mozambique: Approximately 50 SDF personnel joined the U.N. Operation in Mozambique (ONUMOZ) in May 1993 to assist with customs clearance, the allocation of transport means, and the technical coordination of transport. Five of the SDF personnel were assigned as staff officers for ONUMOZ headquarters.

The attitude of the public toward the dispatch of SDF for U.N. peacekeeping operations underwent a significant change. As was stated, when the government proposed the "UN Peace Cooperation Bill" in the midst of the Gulf War, the majority of the public was in opposition to the bill; the poll conducted by the *Asahi Shimbun* indicated that 58 percent were against the bill, while only 21 percent were for it. Opposition to the PKO bill was not so strong. Immediately after the passage of the bill, the public was evenly split; the *Asahi* poll showed that 36 percent were for it, while 36 percent were against it. But after the Cambodian election, the public showed general approval of the PKO law; a *Yomiuri* poll indicated that 55 percent of the public thought highly of the law.[15]

These developments regarding Japan's participation in U.N. peacekeeping are both significant and limited. They are significant by comparison with the virtual nonexistence of Japan's participation in U.N. peace activities before 1989, but they are limited as indicated by the "freeze" of the major peacekeeping activities under the current law. These limitations became even more conspicuous because of the recent developments in the United Nations.

## AFTER CAMBODIA

At about the same time that Japan passed the International Peace Cooperation Bill, U.N. Secretary-General Boutros Boutros-Ghali presented his *An Agenda for Peace*, in which he discussed the possibility of moving beyond the traditional peacekeeping system upon which Japan based its PKO law. What Mr. Boutros-Ghali called "peace enforcement units" posed difficulties for the Japanese because, unless the government changes the interpretation of the Constitution as discussed above, Japanese peacekeepers could not participate in activities that might involve quite frequent "uses of force." Furthermore, developments in Bosnia and Somalia showed that it is quite possible for the U.N. Security Council to allow measures including the "use of force."

Among many in and out of government, there is much skepticism about the way the United Nations is moving in the area of peacekeeping. When Boutros-Ghali's *An Agenda for Peace* was published, it was reported that Prime Minister Miyazawa was uncomfortable with the idea of "peace enforcement units." Foreign Minister Michio Watanabe, when he delivered his speech at the U.N. General Assembly on September 22, 1992, stated:

*Japan believes that the principles and practices of peace-keeping operations upheld by the United Nations for more than 40 years are still both appropriate and valid today and will continue to be so in the future. The idea of "peace-enforcement units," proposed in the Secretary-General's report, offers an interesting approach to future peace-making efforts of the United Nations, but requires further study because it is rooted in a mode of thinking completely different from past peacekeeping forces.[16]*

This skepticism seemed partly derived from a legitimate view that the Secretary-General too easily threw away the principle of "impartiality" for the sake of quick "enforcement"; many wondered whether what worked in the Gulf War could work in civil war situations. But this skepticism was also derived from domestic political inconveniences; now that the government had somehow obtained public support (however limited) for U.N. peacekeeping, it seemed particularly embarrassing for the government to confront the Secretary-General's report, which seemed to consider traditional peacekeeping operations outdated.

## POLITICAL TURMOIL

By the time the SDF mission in Cambodia returned home in September 1993, Japan had plunged into the biggest political turmoil since the LDP consolidated its power in 1955. The disputes within the LDP as well as among the various parties over the issue of political reforms—how to restructure the electoral system and how to tighten political fund regulation—led to the breakup of the LDP and the passage of a vote of no-confidence in June 1993, which brought down the government of Kiichi Miyazawa. Because of the departure of a sizable number of its members from the LDP—one group led by Tsutomu Hata and Ichiro Ozawa and another by Masayoshi Takemura—the LDP was not able to gain a majority in the general election held in mid-July. Ironically, the JSP, the largest opposition party, was the biggest loser; many commentators attributed its failure to the "irresponsible behavior" it displayed during the debate over the PKO bill in the previous year. The Japan New Party, led by Morihiro Hosokawa; *Shinseito* (Renewal Party), led by Hata and Ozawa; and *Sakigake* (the Forerunners), led by Takemura, were the groups that increased their strength in the election. After some maneuvering, to the surprise of many, a coalition was formed to include all small parties except the Communist and the LDP; Morihiro Hosokawa was named the coalition leader and assumed the office of prime minister in August 1993, thus ending the 39-year-long rule of the LDP in Japan.

Although the Hosokawa government attracted widespread popular support—more than 70 percent of the public had a favorable view of it—it was situated on very tenuous ground. The distribution of Diet members revealed two strange characteristics of the coalition government. First, the largest party—the LDP—was out of power, while the coalition government was formed by much smaller parties. Second, even among the coalition partners, the largest party—the JSP—was not in a leading position; Hosokawa was the leader of one of the smallest groups in the coalition. Therefore, the Hosokawa government was naturally suffering from difficulties in dealing with the LDP over Diet maneuvering and in dealing with the JSP over the issue of coalition management.

In addition to difficulties arising from the configuration of power, the coalition government suffered from internal policy differences. The policy goals that bound all coalition partners were their desire to stop the LDP rule first and to achieve some form of political reform second. Even regarding political reform, the coalition partners had difficulties, as was revealed by defections from the JSP over the passage of the political reform bills in late 1993 and early 1994. But over other issues, including tax and security policy, the partners had serious fissures. Reconciliation on tax policy was difficult, but differences over security issues proved to be much more fundamental; the leader of *Shinseito* is Ichiro Ozawa, who has been one of the leading advocates of changing the interpretation of Japan's Constitution to allow U.N. peace operations and a most vocal advocate of the Japan–U.S. alliance, while the largest party in the coalition was the Socialist Party, which had long been the strongest opponent of the SDF, the U.S. alliance, and any dispatch of SDF units abroad even for U.N. operations.

Given these differences, the eventual departure of the Socialists from the coalition in April 1994 may be judged to have been inevitable. Nevertheless, the Socialists, especially their right wing members, have come a long way with respect to Japan's security policy, Japan's relations with the United States, and Japan's relations with the United Nations.

The resignation of Hosokawa following a financial scandal and the brief tenure of Tsutomu Hata led to a period of political turmoil that culminated in a major surprise: the formation of the coalition government of the LDP and the JSP (and *Sakigake*) in late June 1994. It was stunning that a left-wing Socialist, Tomiichi Murayama, was supported by the LDP as its candidate for Prime Minister. This marriage of the archenemies of the Cold War may be explained better by their common hatred against Ichiro Ozawa, the strategist of the *Shinseito* and the main instigator of the political change of 1993, than by any convergence of their views regarding international and domestic policies. Many criticized them for nihilistically making a marriage of sheer political convenience.

But as it turned out, the LDP-JSP-*Sakigake* coalition had more cohesiveness than the previous Hosokawa coalition. Having reached the apex of power for the first time in history, the Socialists, headed by Murayama, made a really historic policy change: They abrogated their traditional policy of "unarmed neutrality." Mr. Murayama said that SDF participation in U.N. peacekeeping operations, which the Socialists had consistently regarded as unconstitutional, is constitutional, and that he "strongly maintains" the Japan-U.S. security framework. The Socialists now support the participation of the SDF in U.N. peacekeeping operations. With this complete about-face, the Socialists' position with respect to international policy became very close to that of the moderate mainstreamers of the LDP. Now that the Cold War is over, the LDP and the Socialists seem to have found other common grounds as well. Both of them have strong rural supporters and are therefore more protectionist than are urban-based political forces. They are not particularly keen on pursuing a "small government." And in international policy, especially with respect to U.N. involvement, they are a rather "passive" participant in peacekeeping operations. To put it differently, their aversion to Japan's active role abroad is much stronger than is that of *Shinseito* supporters.

Therefore, even when Yohei Kono, Foreign Minister of the Murayama government and the President of the LDP, declared Japan's preparedness "to discharge its responsibilities as a permanent member of the Security Council" in September 1994, he also made it clear that "Japan does not, nor will it, resort to the use of force prohibited by its Constitution."[17] This attitude also reflects public opinion. Now the public, with the Socialists, accepts Japan's limited participation in traditional peacekeeping. But when it comes to more forceful action on the part of the United Nations, the public tends to be reluctant. A poll conducted by the *Asahi Shimbun* and three foreign news media (*The New York Times, The Guardian,* and *Der Spiegel*) in April 1994 indicates that only 33 percent of Japanese respondents believe that the United Nations should send armed forces in international conflicts to achieve peace; 50 percent said that the United Nations should not do so. In response to the question of whether Japan has a responsibility to send its armed forces to achieve peace in international conflicts, 50 percent of Japanese respondents denied such responsibility, while only 36 percent answered in the affirmative.[18]

In other words, during the course of the ongoing political change, it has become clear that the extent of Japan's participation in U.N. peace operations—as stipulated in the International Peace Cooperation Law—is a matter of national consensus. Though it is not technically a U.N. peace operation, the dispatch of the SDF for the humanitarian relief mission in Zaire was made by a government headed by a Socialist Prime Minister. Vacillation is still possible, especially when casualties increase. There is still reluctance to dispatch further personnel in additional missions, even if such an action may be appropriate in the current legal framework. But a complete setback is unlikely.

What seems more problematic is whether and to what extent Japan will do more in U.N. peace operations. Concretely speaking, at least two issues are still unresolved. The first is the issue of whether and when Japan will "unfreeze" the "core" missions of the peacekeeping force. If, as Michio Watanabe said at the United Nations in 1993, the principles of U.N peacekeeping are still appropriate and valid, why does Japan continue to "freeze" the most important elements of traditional peacekeeping? The second and more fundamental issue is the relationship between "collective security" and the Japanese Constitution as was raised by Ozawa. If the United Nations is moving toward "peace enforcement" more frequently, should Japan cooperate with such efforts? What kind of "peace-enforcement" operations under Chapter VII of the U.N. Charter should and could Japan fulfill?

As the above analysis indicates, what might be termed "passive participationism" is now prevalent both in the ruling coalition and in the general public. If this tendency continues, the current consensus is the maximum that Japan would do with respect to U.N. peace operations. But the compatibility of the current consensus—

limited participation in traditional U.N. peacekeeping operations—with a country that is seeking a permanent seat in the Security Council is at least problematic. Even if Japan abandons the idea of becoming a permanent member of the Security Council, international developments may not permit the Japanese to avoid difficult decisions indefinitely.

## NOTES

[1]An observation drawn from a joint project to create a database of policy speeches in the Diet by prime ministers and important ministers, funded by the Ministry of Education's Science Research Subsidies. For a preliminary explanation of the database and a tentative compilation of results, see Akihiko Tanaka, "Soridaijin no kokkai enzetsu: detabesu sakusei to tanko shutsugenhindo deta" (Prime Ministers' Diet Speeches: construction of a database and frequency of concept appearance), *Sengo Nihon keisei no kisoteki kenkyu* (Basic Studies of the Formation of the Postwar Japan), Occasional Paper, No. 3 (February 1994).

[2]See Shigeru Kozai, *Kokuren no heiwa iji katsudo* (UN Peacekeeping Operations) (Tokyo: Yuhikaku 1991), pp. 475-77.

[3]The major motive behind this resolution was not to counter the possibility of sending troops abroad for U.N. missions but to prohibit any attempt to send troops for collective self-defense purposes under the U.S.-Japan security arrangements. See ibid., pp. 478-82.

[4]Ibid., pp. 485-86.

[5]Ibid., p. 487.

[6]*Boei handobukku Heisei 6 nenban* (Defense Handbook 1994) (Tokyo: Asagumo Shimbunsha, 1994), p. 407. One significant difference between this interpretation and the previous interpretation as represented by Mr. Hayashi was that this interpretation used "the use of force" as the single most important criterion to differentiate "UN force." The 1961 interpretation by Hayashi and the interpretation by Mr. Takatsuji, the succeeding Director General of the Cabinet Legislation Bureau to Mr. Hayashi, referred to the possibility of "an ideal form" of U.N. force. This possibility was not at all mentioned in the 1980 interpretation. See Seiki Nishihiro, "Seifu no anpo toben no hensen" (Evolution of the Government's Statements as to Security) in Yomiuri Shimbunsha Chosakenkyuhonbu, *Kenpo o kangaeru* (Thinking About the Constitution) (Tokyo: Yomiuri Shimbunsha, 1993), pp. 59-81.

[7]In fact, a Komeito representative criticized the government for this recommendation. But in comparison with the intensity of debate after the Gulf War, this episode was almost insignificant; no public debates followed in any case. See Kozai, op cit., p. 502.

[8]*Diplomatic Bluebook 1988*, p. 26.

[9]In my chapter of a book published in April 1990, I argued for the desirability of Japan's participation in U.N. peacekeeping activities. But I remember that very few who read the manuscript showed interest in such an idea. See Akihiko Tanaka, "Badon Shearingu" (Burden-sharing) in Mitsuo Mastushita and Makoto Kuroda, eds. *Nihon to Amerika-21seiki he no shinario* (Japan and America: a scenario for the 21st century) (Tokyo: PHP, 1990), pp. 80-102.

[10]Akihiko Tanaka, "Soridaijin no kokkaienzetsu."

[11]Quoted in Sasaki, *Umiokoeru Jieitai* (SDF Going Abroad) (Tokyo: Iwanami, 1992), p. 14.

[12]*Boei handobuku heisei 6 nenban*, pp. 408-09.

[13]Ibid., p. 410.

[14]*Diplomatic Bluebook 1992*, p. 53.

[15]See Naoto Nonaka, "PKO kyoryokuhoan wo meguru kokunai seiji katei to Nihon gaiko" (Domestic Political Process of PKO Bill and Japan's Diplomacy) in Nihon Keizai Kyogikai, *Kokuren kaikaku to Nihon* (U.N. Reform and Japan) (Tokyo: Nihon Keizai Kyogikai, 1994), p. 50.

[16]Ibid., pp. 439-40.

[17]Permanent Mission of Japan to the United Nations, "Statement by H.E. Mr. Yohei Kono, Deputy Prime Minister and Minister for Foreign Affairs of Japan at the 49th Session of the General Assembly of the United Nations," *Press Release* (September 27, 1994).

[18]*Asahi Shimbun*, April 2, 1994. This response pattern of the Japanese is in stark contrast with those of their counterparts in the United States, Great Britain, and Germany. In the latter countries, the majority was in favor of U.N. armed activities in conflict areas and felt that their countries have responsibilities to send troops for such missions.

# Annex

## MISSIONS UNDER THE INTERNATIONAL PEACE COOPERATION LAW

### [U.N. Peacekeeping Operations]

1. Monitoring the observance of cessation of armed conflict and relation, withdrawal, or demobilization of armed forces
2. Stationing and patrolling in buffer zones
3. Inspection or identification of the carrying in or out of weapons
4. Collection, storage, or disposal of abandoned weapons
5. Assistance for the designation of ceasefire lines and other boundaries by the parties to armed conflicts
6. Assistance for the exchange of prisoners of war among the parties to armed conflicts
7. Medical care (including sanitary measures)
8. Transportation, communication, construction, etc.
9. Supervision or management of fair execution of elections or voting
10. Advice or guidance for and supervision of police administrative matters
11. Advice or guidance for administrative matters not covered by 10 (above)

### [Humanitarian International Relief Operation]

12. Search or rescue of affected people or assistance for their repatriation
13. Distribution of food, clothing, medical supplies, and other daily necessities to affected people and medical care for them
14. Installation of facilities or equipment to accommodate affected people
15. Measures for the repair or maintenance of facilities or equipment necessary for the daily lives of affected people
16. Restoration and other measures of facilities and the natural environment subjected to damages by conflicts

Notes: Items 1 through 6 are regarded as the "core" functions of peacekeeping forces and are currently "frozen." Items 9 and 10 are functions conducted by civilian personnel.

Source: *Defense of Japan 1993*, p. 130.

EDWARD C.
LUCK

# 3

TAKAKO
UETA

# LAYERS OF SECURITY:

## REGIONAL ARRANGEMENTS, THE UNITED NATIONS, AND THE JAPAN–U.S. SECURITY TREATY

| EDWARD C. LUCK | LAYERS OF SECURITY: REGIONAL ARRANGEMENTS, THE UNITED NATIONS, AND THE JAPAN–U.S. SECURITY TREATY |

The end of the Cold War has prompted a rethinking of strategic priorities, security alignments, and multilateral arrangements throughout the world. These reassessments are cutting deepest in Eastern Europe, where the NATO/ Warsaw Pact confrontation has undergone a rapid meta- morphosis. In East Asia, where the East-West rivalry was less starkly defined and the Soviet Union was only one of several major powers, the ripple effects of the Soviet collapse have been more subtle in the short run. Over time, however, questions about the possibility of new regional arrangements, the role of the United Nations in Asian affairs, and the future of the U.S.-Japan Security Treaty are being posed with increasing frequency. These questions arise at a time when the four major powers in East Asia—the United States, Japan, China, and Russia—are all undergoing important changes in their domestic political orders that could alter their foreign policy priorities. The United Nations, on the eve of its fiftieth anniversary, is itself going through a period of transition, reflection, and perhaps, redefinition. For Japan, as it considers the benefits and responsibilit- ies of permanent membership in the U.N. Security Council and debates the degree of its participation in U.N. peacekeeping, these issues are central to the future of its foreign and security policies.

This paper addresses the complex interactions among three critical elements of East Asian security: possible regional security arrangements, U.N. peace operations, and the U.S.-Japan Security Treaty. It begins with a broad discussion of the legal relationships between global and regional bodies set out five decades ago by the drafters of the U.N. Charter, then considers the continuing role of the U.S.-Japan Security Treaty, and concludes with some thoughts about the role of East Asia in the United Nations, about the role of the United Nations in East Asia, and about possible regional arrangements. It argues that efforts on all levels—unilateral Japanese and U.S. defense preparations, the bilateral security rela- tionship, regional arrangements, and the United Nations—can, and should, be pursued in a mutually supportive and reinforcing manner. There is no need to choose among them, since they can be crafted to be complementary, not competitive, means to bolster regional stability. In each crisis, the mix of tools employed will depend on the circumstances and the preferences of U.S. and Japanese leaders, so it is important to preserve a wide range of credible policy options. The ultimate goal should be to achieve a sensible balance—a division of labor—among these different layers of security in a way that maximizes the mutual security interests of the United States and Japan without threatening the security of others in the region.

## THE UNITED NATIONS AND REGIONAL ORGANIZATIONS: REDISCOVERING CHAPTER VIII

The U.N. Charter envisioned a very different collective security system than what exists today. It was to be more robust, more integrated, and more systematic, with a series of interdependent layers. Chapter VI of the Charter outlines possibilities for non-coercive peacemaking, Chapter VII details a range of Security Council-authorized enforcement measures, and Chapter VIII presents related regional arrangements that would complement and bolster U.N. peace and security efforts. With a few notable exceptions, the Security Council could rarely agree on any steps beyond Chapter VI during the Cold War years. Traditional peacekeeping was invented as a creative extension of non-coercive diplomacy, under what is often referred to as Chapter VI$\frac{1}{2}$. The end of Cold War bickering in the Council has permitted a rediscovery of the coercive powers— if not the machinery[1]—of Chapter VII. The third leg of the collective security triad, Chapter VIII, remains largely dormant, unexplored territory. Though U.N. Secretary-General Boutros Boutros-Ghali has long had a personal interest in the role of regional organizations and devoted substantial space to the subject in his 1992 *An Agenda for Peace*, it remains the least studied and least understood aspect of the Charter's vision.[2]

Over the years, the Security Council has become the first stop in trying to resolve any number of domestic, local, and regional conflicts, but that was not the original intention. According to Article 33 of Chapter VI, "the parties to any dispute, the continuance of which is likely to endanger the maintenance of international peace and security, shall, *first of all*, seek a solution by negotiation, enquiry, mediation, conciliation, arbitration, judicial settlement, *resort to regional agencies or arrangements*, or other peaceful means of their own choice" [emphasis added]. Should these efforts under Article 33 fail to settle the dispute, continues Article 37, then the parties "shall refer it to the Security Council."

Chapter VIII is even more explicit on this point. Article 52, paragraph 1, underlines that "nothing in the present Charter precludes the existence of regional arrangements or agencies for dealing with such matters relating to the maintenance of international peace and security as are appropriate for regional action, provided that such arrangements or agencies and their activities are consistent with the Purposes and Principles of the United Nations." Paragraph 2 states that "the Members of the United Nations entering into such arrangements or constituting such agencies shall make every effort to achieve pacific settlement of local disputes through such regional arrangements or by such regional agencies *before* referring them to the Security Council" [emphasis added]. Paragraph 3 calls on the Council to "encourage the development of pacific settlement of local disputes through such regional arrangements or by such regional agencies."

The Security Council, in other words, in most cases was to be the final recourse, not the first one. Regional organizations were to act as a buffer or filter, sorting through and addressing where possible local security problems, with the Council getting involved directly only when lower levels could not handle the trouble. Instead of lurching from crisis to crisis, as it does today, the Council could play more of an oversight or supervisory role if regional organizations were up to the task assigned to them by the Charter. Instead of being flooded with an ever-growing list of local atrocities and conflicts—the resolutions of most of which lie beyond the interests, will, and capabilities of the permanent members—the Council could devote appropriate reflection and deliberation to those major threats to international peace and security where a broad consensus is in prospect or the need for collective action appears to be especially urgent.

Given the frenetic pace of Security Council work these days, the Council members would be hard pressed to sustain the degree of concentrated attention and effort that they devoted, for example, to Iraq's invasion of Kuwait in the six months prior to Desert Storm and following the conclusion of the fighting. A more reflective and deliberate decision-making process, backed by a small policy planning staff, moreover, might help the Council to avoid some of the ill-conceived or inconsistent resolutions that have plagued the

Bosnia and Somalia missions. By taking on so many crises simultaneously and by churning out words much faster than deeds, the members of the Council have seriously undermined the credibility of the world's foremost security mechanism in recent years. For example, the Council has now produced more than 110 statements and resolutions on the crisis in the former Yugoslavia—a number of them inconsistent or contradictory—as if words could substitute for action.

Regional organizations, on the other hand, are least developed where they are most needed. In areas of perennial tension, such as the Middle East, the Persian Gulf, and South Asia, deep-seated political differences have precluded the cooperative relationships on which effective regional cooperation must be based. As will be discussed below, it is understandable—though increasingly regrettable—that the development of regional mechanisms has never gotten beyond the talking stage in Northeast Asia. In these areas, the lack of regional arrangements that could play a preventive or mediating role means that there is no alternative to turning first to the Security Council if multilateral cooperation is sought to handle a dispute or conflict, such as the ongoing crisis over nuclear developments in North Korea. The Council, of course, has legal authority to take enforcement action binding on all 185 member states. This degree of authority, unprecedented in human history, is unlikely to be duplicated on the regional level, and certainly not in East Asia and other regions where cooperative relationships are at an early stage of development. The constraints are political and practical, not legal. The Charter foresaw a division of labor in which regional arrangements and agencies could take a range of diplomatic and enforcement actions under the Council's ultimate authority that, in turn, would ease its burden.

The debacle in Bosnia-Herzegovina provides ample evidence that even the existence of relatively strong regional security, legal, and political bodies, such as in Europe, is no guarantee of effective collective efforts in every crisis. NATO and the Organization on Security and Cooperation in Europe (OSCE) have been just as divided and ambivalent about how to handle the conflict as has been the Security Council. For historic, strategic, and political reasons, countries in the neighborhood may be more likely to have differing perspectives and interests than would those nations on the Council that are farther removed geographically, historically, and psychologically from the conflict. In theory, the Council's distance from the scene is often one of its primary assets. In practice, the nations most willing to intervene or to provide forces for U.N. missions—whether Russia in Georgia, the United States in Haiti, or France in Rwanda—are those that believe that they have a national interest in the outcome of the local strife.

In the case of the disintegration of the former Yugoslavia, repeated attempts to work out a sensible division of labor among the United Nations, NATO, and other European regional bodies have failed to work out fully satisfactory relationships between global and regional efforts to resolve the crisis. Institutional interests, personality clashes, and differing perspectives have inevitably complicated matters at crucial points, recalling the old adage that where one stands depends on where one sits. But more fundamentally, the international response to the tragedy in Bosnia-Herzegovina makes it abundantly clear that no collective effort can overcome the indecision, hesitancy, and weak will of the key member states. Multilateralism has never been able to substitute for national strength and determination—indeed, it must be built on them—and that will be just as true for East Asia.

Chapter VIII of the U.N. Charter never defines regional "arrangements and agencies," many of which were developed years after the Charter was implemented, often with the impetus of the Cold War.[3] Some regional organizations, such as the OSCE and the Organization of American States (OAS), have explicitly defined themselves as regional organizations under Chapter VIII. The series of alliances or security pacts developed during the Cold War to protect one group of states against another—such as NATO, the Warsaw Pact, or the U.S.-Japan security relationship—however, have chosen not to label themselves as Chapter VIII organizations. This is understandable, since each of these security pacts was intended to guard against potential aggression by one or more of the permanent members of the Security Council. Article 53 stresses that "no enforcement action shall be taken under regional arrangements or by regional agencies without the authorization of the Security Council,"[4] and Article 54 states that the Council "shall at all times be kept fully informed" of peace and security efforts by regional groups. Given these conditions, it is evident that the employment of Chapter VIII organizations against the interests, allies, forces, or territory of any of the permanent members of the Council was not anticipated, since they could veto any such action. Now that they have become the five declared nuclear powers, as well as the five largest arms exporters, this would also appear to be a limitation on collective security under the United Nations—and it makes sense from a military, as well as a political, perspective. Clearly, neither the United Nations nor regional organizations associated with it are positioned to intervene in conflicts among or involving the permanent members.

For political more than material reasons, the Security Council has frequently sought to work with regional organizations in collaborative efforts to resolve conflicts through peaceful means. This has sometimes been true even when a militarily powerful permanent member, such as the United States in Haiti, has dominated the international effort. Examples of global-regional cooperation have included joint U.N. undertakings with the Contadora Group and the OAS in Central America, the Association of South-East Asian Nations (ASEAN) in Cambodia, and the Organization of African Unity (OAU) in Southern Rhodesia, Namibia, South Africa, Eritrea, and Mozambique. Perhaps the most promising collaboration has been in election monitoring and related nation-building efforts in places such as El Salvador, Mozambique, and Haiti.

The collaborative record in situations requiring coercive measures under Chapter VII, however, has been much more spotty. The OAU sought unsuccessfully to enlist U.N. financial and political support for an African military mission to end the civil war in Chad.[5] The Economic Community of Western African States was widely accused of taking sides when it intervened in the Liberian civil war, and the Security Council agreed to send a small force only in the latter stages of the ongoing conflict. The Arab League declined to take part in Operation Desert Storm in Kuwait, and the OAU role in Somalia, Angola, and Rwanda has been marginal. The OAU did back the Tanzanian-led overthrow of Idi Amin's reign of terror in Uganda, since the United Nations was less prepared in those days to intervene in a nation's "internal affairs" no matter how repressive or repugnant the regime.

Since Chapter VIII organizations tend to be regional political groupings rather than military alliances, it is understandable that they have generally not taken part in coercive military operations under Chapter VII. Even if they give their political backing to such steps, they lack the command structure and patterns of military cooperation required for effective joint-combat operations. It is awkward, moreover, for regional organizations to appear to be taking sides in civil conflicts within their areas.

As NATO's uneven and ultimately disappointing experience trying to enforce Security Council–defined missions in Bosnia demonstrates, even the most powerful military alliance may not be in a good position to act as the regional military wing of the Security Council. In this case, an alliance formed to counter the expansion of the influence of a permanent member of the Council has necessarily lacked the political breadth to represent the Council as a whole in combat. What might have been the first case of Russian-American cooperation in U.N. enforcement efforts in the post–Cold War era has turned into a confusing competition for influence. Coordination on military matters between NATO and the United Nations has proven problematic. While three of the Council's permanent members also have been the NATO members most involved in enforcement efforts in Bosnia, there have proven to be troubling gaps in the institutional cultures and attitudes of the two organizations. At times it has seemed that either everyone or no one was in charge of this essentially dual-key (or mutual veto) command structure.

The drafters of the Charter had something quite different in mind. Article 47 of Chapter VII calls for the establishment of "a Military Staff Committee to advise and assist the Security Council on all questions relating to the Security Council's military requirements for the maintenance of international peace and security, the employment and command of forces placed at its disposal, the regulation of armaments, and possible disarmament." Made up of the Chiefs of Staff of the permanent members and of other member states "when the efficient discharge of the Committee's responsibilities requires," the Committee was to provide "strategic direction of any forces placed at the disposal of the Security Council." Questions of actual command of the forces, however, were to "be worked out subsequently." While the Military Staff Committee continues to meet regularly at a low level, Cold War tensions followed by post–Cold War uncertainties have prevented it from playing any substantive role in planning or conducting U.N. peace operations.[6]

Paragraph 4 of Article 47 gives the Military Staff Committee the power to "establish regional sub-committees" with the authorization of the Security Council and "after consultation with appropriate regional agencies." In essence, this long-forgotten clause permits the Committee to create regional military groupings to help the Security Council carry out its wide-ranging responsibilities for arms control, disarmament, and economic and military enforcement measures under Chapter VII. This step could have been very helpful politically, if less so militarily, in bolstering regional support for the operations in Somalia and Iraq. The implementation and monitoring of trade embargoes imposed by the Security Council— as in the cases of Iraq, Libya, and Serbia/Montengro and as may have been the case with North Korea—also frequently require the cooperation of naval or other military units from the region.

In the current generation of U.N. peace operations, which tend to have much broader mandates than traditional peacekeeping, competent military planning is often needed for the enforcement of economic sanctions, for the implementation of arms control and disarmament measures, and for the organization of the delivery of humanitarian assistance on a massive scale. Frequently undertaken in hostile or chaotic environments, these operations are defined and carried out in ways that blur the distinctions between Chapters VI and VII, which confuses publics and legislators alike. While the United States and a few other major powers have unique and essential military assets to provide to U.N. peace operations, some of the most ambitious nation-building missions—such as those in Cambodia, El Salvador, and Namibia—have also relied on the political, diplomatic, and material contributions of countries from the region. In Haiti, where U.S. forces faced only nominal military opposition, the political backing of local countries—many of them quite small—was treated by Washington as an essential foundation for a successful intervention.

## THE UNITED NATIONS AND THE JAPAN–U.S. SECURITY TREATY

The United Nations Charter, completed while World War II was still under way and before the explosion of the first atomic bomb, pre-dates the establishment of the network of bilateral and regional alliances that defined security during four decades of Cold War. With the collapse of the Soviet Union and the re-emergence of the United Nations as a potential instrument of collective security, pundits and policy analysts in Japan, Western Europe, and the United States are questioning the future roles and even the relevance of the alliances that were formed to counter a potentially aggressive power that no longer exists, or that at least is only a shadow of its former self. While NATO has been the focus for much of this re-evaluation, the shape and future of the bilateral security relationship between the United States and Japan is also being re-examined under changing circumstances. The process of reassessment, in my view, should lead both parties to recommit themselves to the bilateral treaty as an essential building block for enhanced multilateral cooperation in the region and with the United Nations. The bilateral security relationship reinforces East Asian stability and security, serving itself as a confidence-building measure. Article I of the Treaty of Mutual Cooperation and Security Between Japan and the United States of America, moreover, refers to strengthening the United Nations as one of its primary purposes, while through repeated references it makes clear that its provisions are firmly rooted in the framework of the U.N. Charter.

The collective security mechanisms of the United Nations, on the other hand, clearly cannot substitute for a strong bilateral alliance in terms of meeting the fundamental defense needs of Japan. For the foreseeable future, the protection of the home islands and of supply routes for essential resources can be attained only through a combination of adequate Japanese Self-Defense Forces (SDF) and the deterrent provided by American guarantees backed by forward-deployed U.S. conventional and nuclear forces. With no forces of its own, the United Nations must rely on militarily significant member states to contribute sufficient forces to implement the mandates laid down by the Security Council. So even if the bilateral security treaty did not exist, Japan and the United Nations would have to look to U.S. forces to help repulse a major assault on Japan or the essential sea lanes. No other country has the power-projection capabilities, much less the will, to get the job done. Neither Japan nor the United States can afford to believe in the fantasy that the United Nations will provide their security for them or that the revival of the United Nations in itself means that they can significantly reduce their defense efforts. The opposite may be the case, at least in the short run.

Members of Congress have increasingly complained in recent months about their perception that support for U.N. peace operations draws down the general readiness of U.S. forces and puts an extra burden on the defense budget. They are seeking offsetting reductions in U.S. assessments for U.N. peacekeeping missions. By multiplying the number of conflicts in which U.S. forces are involved at least indirectly, the expansion of U.N. peacekeeping and enforcement commitments around the world could actually increase the demand for some kinds of U.S. conventional military capabilities such as airlift, sealift, mine clearing, special forces, military police, and logistics support. The same can be said, to a lesser degree, for the SDF.

The United Nations cannot be strong if its key member states are weak, whether in military, political, or economic terms. Through its multilateral decision-making mechanisms, the United Nations does offer a route toward more equitable burden-sharing and toward enhanced political legitimacy for international military missions. But the United Nations has no capabilities for reducing the overall burden of collective security when aggressors and parties to a conflict resist its efforts at peaceful mediation and conciliation. When the weakness of a state tempts aggression on the part of more powerful neighbors or leads to internal collapse, it only adds to the U.N.'s burden in seeking to maintain international peace and security. As Article 51 emphasizes, "nothing in the present Charter shall impair the inherent right of individual or collective self-defense if an armed attack occurs against a Member of the United Nations, until the Security Council has taken measures necessary to maintain international peace and security."

Not only are self-defense measures considered legitimate under Article 51, but member states with the resources to do so have an implicit obligation under the Charter to maintain some supplemental forces to commit to the Security Council–authorized defense of other nations less capable of providing sufficiently for their own security or for that of their peoples. Otherwise, the United States and other militarily powerful countries would have to carry a disproportionate burden of global security and the U.N.'s conflict resolution work would itself be hampered by the absence of any credible deterrent to aggressive actions. Under the Charter, the Secretary-General and his secretariat are to play the "good cop" mediation roles described in Chapter VI, while the member states— especially the permanent members—are called upon to exercise the "bad cop" enforcement functions of Chapter VII.

It should also be recalled, as noted above, that the rules of the Security Council virtually exclude the possibility of U.N. action against one of the permanent members—unless they are boycotting the Council at the time, as the Soviet Union was when the 1950 Korean operation was approved—or their allies. The three major powers with the military potential—at least hypothetically—to pose a substantial threat to the Japanese homeland at some point in the future—the United States, Russia, and China—are all permanent members of the Security Council with veto power over its actions.[7] While none of these powers has any motivation for or intention of threatening Japan in the foreseeable future, neither the revival of the United Nations nor Japanese permanent membership on the Security Council could provide reliable security guarantees for Japan should conditions change for the worse in the future. It is the security treaty with the United States and the maintenance of adequate SDF that will provide an effective deterrent no matter what leadership changes take place in China and Russia.

It is striking, in any case, that in a recent survey more Japanese respondents named the United States than any other country as "the biggest threat to world peace."[8] The United States, at 22 percent, was followed closely by Russia (21 percent) and North Korea (13 percent). While polls are not always considered reliable in Japan, and the response probably reflected economic more than military tensions, concerted efforts are clearly needed to reinforce public support for the alliance.[9] With keen competition on trade issues probably inevitable between the world's two largest economies, it is doubly important that the security and political ties between Tokyo and Washington remain close and above the fray of economic rivalry. Their security relationship has provided both a framework and a foundation for the stability that has allowed Asia to prosper largely outside of the East-West military competition. The unraveling of the U.S.-Japan Security Treaty would have far-reaching and unpredictable consequences for relationships among the four major powers in East Asia—the United States, Japan, China, and Russia—all of which are going through periods of uncertainty and transition in national leadership, domestic priorities, and foreign policy. It could lead to a more pacifist or a more militarist Japan, neither of which is a desirable outcome in terms of international stability and Japanese domestic tranquility.

## ASIA IN THE UNITED NATIONS AND THE UNITED NATIONS IN ASIA

Just as it is essential for East Asian security that the United States remain fully engaged militarily, politically, and economically in the region, it is essential that Japan play a larger role in global security if it wants to be accorded a higher, and more appropriate, place in the U.N. hierarchy. Permanent members of the Security Council, with its worldwide responsibilities and expanding agenda, have to take positions on how the United Nations should deal with crises far from home on a daily basis. The four-nation public opinion survey cited above, however, confirms the continuing Asian orientation of the Japanese people. When asked who other than the United States is "the strongest candidate for world leadership," 38 percent of Japanese named China, 24 percent Japan, and only 12 percent Western Europe. Americans, on the other hand, took a more balanced approach, citing China 25 percent of the time, Japan 28 percent, and Western Europe 26 percent.[10] The Japanese, moreover, seem somewhat less worried about international security trends than do Americans, perhaps because most of the current chaos appears far away. By a 37 to 26 percent margin, Japanese respondents said that the world had become more dangerous rather than safer since the end of the Cold War. The ratio in the United States, however, was almost 3-to-1, with 67 percent saying the world has become more dangerous and 24 percent responding that it is safer now.

Despite the Japanese government's concerted efforts to overcome public misgivings about participation in U.N. peacekeeping operations, the public's willingness to be involved still lags significantly behind attitudes in other countries. For example, the four-nation survey cited above found Americans by more than a 2-to-1 majority agreeing that the United Nations should "send military troops to enforce peace plans in trouble spots around the world," while 50 percent of Japanese respondents said that the United Nations should *not* do so, and only 33 percent said that it should. When asked whether their country "has a responsibility to contribute military troops" to such an operation, only 36 percent of Japanese respondents agreed, compared with 59 percent of the Americans polled. Somewhat more surprisingly, given how controversial the United Nations has been in the United States—particularly in Congress—Americans responded somewhat more positively than did the Japanese to the question of whether "the United Nations has contributed to keeping world peace in the last 50 years."[11]

According to Article 23 of the Charter, the first criterion for election to the Security Council is supposed to be contributions "to the maintenance of international peace and security." Nothing is said about having a global perspective, but the latter helps when so much of the Council's attention is drawn to conflicts far from East Asia. If Japan and Germany are seen as essentially regional powers, not global players, there will be less support in the U.N.

diplomatic community for their ascension to permanent seats in the Council. Already, developing countries are complaining about the overly narrow focus of the current permanent members and their reluctance to get involved directly in civil conflicts in places like Rwanda, Liberia, and Angola. In this context, Japan's participation, however modest, in U.N. missions in places where it has no apparent national interest—such as Mozambique and Rwanda—has been most welcome.

As a frequent non-permanent member of the Council, Japan has voted publicly on any number of controversies around the world without creating a storm of protest at home or straining its relations with the United States. On some issues, such as in the Middle East, Japanese and American positions have often diverged. As long as their bilateral political and security ties remain strong, differences between the United States and Japan on some global issues will be taken in stride, without damage to the overall relationship. If Japan gains the veto power at a time when relations between Tokyo and Washington are already tense because of trade or other differences, however, things could get complicated. For example, what if Japan had had a permanent seat and veto power in mid-1994 when the United States was pressing for economic sanctions against North Korea because of its nuclear program? Would Japan have threatened a veto to satisfy its economic and domestic interests at the risk of angering the United States on a central security matter? As it was, Japan seemed to possess a tacit veto—even though it was not even a member of the Council at the time—since its cooperation would have been essential to implementing any sanctions regime.

Through the years, the work of the Security Council has tended to be dominated by the United States and essentially European powers (the Soviet Union/Russia, France, and the United Kingdom). China, the only Asian permanent member, has usually played a modest, defensive, and reactive role. For obvious reasons, Beijing has generally been unenthusiastic about the application of sanctions, fretting about threats to sovereignty and about interference in essentially domestic affairs. On controversial security issues, China has generally focused more on negotiations over the wording of proposed resolutions than on trying to sway the voting itself. The goal for China at times seems to be to produce wording vague enough that it does not feel compelled to veto the resolution and to ruin a broad Western-led consensus, since it apparently prefers to abstain on something a bit unattractive rather than to veto something truly obnoxious to Chinese views.

In terms of supplying troops for U.N. peacekeeping operations, India, Pakistan, and Bangladesh have been far more active participants than have either China or Japan, although Tokyo's tortured decision to begin to provide modest SDF contingents for support roles in U.N. missions in Cambodia, Mozambique, and Zaire (to assist Rwandan refugees) has been widely appreciated in the U.N. community as a step in the right direction. This initiative, along with Japan's longstanding efforts on nuclear proliferation, a test ban, a conventional arms transfer registry, and other arms control measures, certainly qualifies as "a contribution to the maintenance of international peace and security." Moreover, Japan's financial support for a wide range of U.N. activities, including the Cambodian operation, has been substantial and growing. Tokyo has found it difficult, however, to translate these financial contributions into political capital within the U.N. system, especially on the peace and security side. With Yasushi Akashi having led U.N. peace efforts in Cambodia and now in the former Yugoslavia, and with Sadako Ogata serving as the U.N. High Commissioner for Refugees, Japanese personalities are for the first time in key positions to shape high-profile missions. Japan has certainly moved a long way toward becoming a "normal" member state in the United Nations.

Not only have East Asian countries kept a relatively low profile in the United Nations on security issues, but the United Nations has been involved less in East Asian affairs than in any region other than North America. Most U.N. peace operations have taken place in parts of the developing world, primarily in Africa, the Middle East, South Asia, and Central America, where Japan's political and security roles have been minimal (and only in the Middle East is its interest—oil—substantial). With four major powers involved in East Asian security, three of them permanent members of the Council, there has been little room for consensus in the Security Council on how to proceed in the region. Likewise, this political mix has prevented the nations of East Asia from acting as a bloc in the General Assembly and other large U.N. deliberative bodies, which has further constrained their influence. The relatively stable security environment, moreover, bolstered by the American presence, has meant that there have been relatively few crises in East Asia that required U.N. intervention. And the region's prosperity has kept it from being a candidate for major U.N. development projects.

The current crisis regarding North Korea's apparent nuclear ambitions is a major exception. For the first time in four decades, tensions in East Asia are near the top of the Security Council's priority list. The statute of the International Atomic Energy Agency requires that the Agency bring to the Council's attention cases of possible safeguards violations; but in the absence of any broad-based (or Chapter VIII) regional security arrangements in East Asia, there was nowhere else to bring the complaint in any case. While there have been many tracts written in recent years on possible confidence- and security-building measures for the region,[12] there is no institutional framework within which to develop and implement such steps in East Asia. There is no institutional buffer, in other words, between bilateral relations and the U.N. Security Council should tensions escalate. This could be a recipe for trouble, despite the Asian penchant for informal discussion as a means of easing tensions.

There have been dozens of proposals through the years, of course, for Asian regional cooperative arrangements based on European models.[13] Many of these were concocted in Moscow and were therefore non-starters in Washington and Tokyo. At no point have all four major powers in the region been on good terms and perceived an Asian political framework to be in their national interests at the same time. There have been problems of geographical definition, since the security problems of Southeast Asia are quite distinct from those of Northeast Asia. With four major and many smaller powers in East Asia, it has not been evident how countries of very disparate sizes could work together in a shared forum, although the OSCE and the United Nations are quite familiar with this problem. As long as the security environment remains relatively stable and there are no major crises, moreover, the motivation for establishing regional arrangements will not be compelling.

With the collapse of the Soviet Union, China's growing market orientation, fresh dynamics on the Korean Peninsula, and Japan's emergence as a political, security, and economic power, the time is ripe for revisiting the issue of regional arrangements in East Asia. Until the Chinese leadership succession is settled, of course, the nature of new arrangements cannot be finalized, but now is a good time to begin to test the political waters and to float some trial balloons. These efforts should be pursued on two levels, neither of which would require a complicated organization or a large bureaucracy. The first would be a quadrilateral dialogue among the four major powers—the United States, Japan, China, and Russia—on their defense plans and concerns, on their perceptions of the evolving Asian strategic environment, and on potential flash points in the region, including both Southeast and Northeast Asia, and possibly South Asia as well.[14] In light of China's broad military modernization program, a candid exchange on defense issues could help ease misapprehensions and foster much-needed transparency. In the long run, the ties established through such an exchange could improve quadrilateral communications in future crises, especially if the discussions included top military as well as political leaders. The possibility of establishing a four-sided "hot line" could be floated. The agenda should include a wide range of emerging security problems, such as disputes in the South China Sea, North Korea's nuclear program and political stability, and possibly the future of Taiwan, as well as defense plans and doctrines.

A second avenue, widely discussed in recent years, would be an East Asia–wide political and security dialogue. Confidence- and security-building measures would be high on its agenda. A number of observers have suggested a conference on security and cooperation in Asia, patterned after the Conference on Security and Cooperation in Europe (now the OSCE). While recently it has gained a more developed institutional superstructure, for many years the CSCE, without a substantial bureaucracy or formal powers, proved to be a helpful bridge between East and West. Similar bridges might be handy in East Asia as well, although there the ideological divides are much less sharp and the degree of economic and social interaction far more advanced.

There is also talk of extending fundamentally economic groupings—either the Asia-Pacific Economic Cooperation (APEC) forum or ASEAN—into the political and security realms. In July 1994, the ASEAN Regional Forum was launched, including Japan, China, Russia, South Korea, and the United States along with the ASEAN countries.[15] Whether an initiative of the relatively small nations of Southeast Asia can realistically address the problems of Northeast Asia or draw in the major powers on important peace and security issues remains to be seen. The two Koreas may well feel that this is an inappropriate place to discuss their sensitive relationship. APEC has the advantage of strong U.S. backing since its inception, but it has focused on economic questions and includes Taiwan, which is a problematic feature from the Chinese perspective if political and security issues are to be considered.

Any effort at regional organization in the Asia-Pacific region will face both difficult problems of geographical definition and enormous disparities in the region. The precise form such an arrangement might take, however, is less important than that the momentum toward regional cooperation on peace and security issues be maintained and then accelerated. The time is propitious for creating the kind of regional arrangements envisioned under Chapter VIII: those involving broad regional cooperation on arms control, conflict resolution, confidence-building, and peacekeeping with an eye toward regional stability and the maintenance of peace, not the containment of an adversary. The purpose would be conflict prevention, not enforcement, with the regional efforts aimed at easing the burdens on the Security Council rather than at usurping the Council's ultimate political authority and enforcement powers. Combined with adequate Japanese and American defense preparations, strong bilateral security ties, and a revived and expanded U.N. Security Council, the process of regional cooperation can add the missing element in the architecture for a stable future for East Asia.

## NOTES

[1]For commentary on the command and control problems caused by the failure to observe Chapter VII procedures in Bosnia and Somalia, see Edward C. Luck, "This Isn't the Way to Have the United Nations Keep the Peace," *International Herald Tribune*, April 19, 1994.

[2]The conclusions of *An Agenda for Peace* in this regard were themselves rather general. Noting that "today a new sense exists that they [regional organizations] have contributions to make" toward peace within their regions, the Secretary-General called for expanded consultations between the United Nations and regional bodies and for "complementary efforts" and "joint undertakings" between the two levels of international organization. Boutros Boutros-Ghali, *An Agenda for Peace* (New York: United Nations, 1992), p. 37.

[3]Two regional arrangements, the Arab League and the Rio Pact, were concluded just prior to the founding of the United Nations to underline their autonomous identities.

[4]Paragraph 1 of Article 53 continues with an important exception "of measures against any enemy state," defined in paragraph 2 as "any state which during the Second World War has been an enemy of any signatory of the present Charter." This archaic caveat is further elaborated in Article 107. While this so-called "enemies clause" would have no practical effect in the real world, it might hinder the development of a Chapter VIII organization in East Asia. With the prospect of Japan and Germany becoming permanent members of the Security Council at

some point, with or without a veto, it is doubly important to eliminate this historic relic from the Charter.

[5]For a case study, see I. William Zartman, "Conflict in Chad," in Arthur R. Day and Michael W. Doyle, eds., *Escalation and Intervention: Multilateral Security and Its Alternatives* (Boulder, Colorado: Westview Press, 1986).

[6]For the recommendations of a Russian-American task force on how the Military Staff Committee role could be recast and enhanced in the post-Cold War era, see *When Diplomacy Fails: Russian-American Proposals for United Nations Military Action* (New York: The United Nations Association of the USA, the Center for National Security and International Relations (Moscow), and the United Nations Association of the Russian Federation) January 31, 1994.

[7]Likewise, should Japan and Germany gain vetoes along with permanent seats in the Security Council, they would be in a position to block U.N. enforcement action in their regions and around the world. For this reason, some of their neighbors might prefer that the two countries not be granted veto power as well as permanent seats on the Council.

[8]From a four-nation poll—United States, Japan, United Kingdom, and Germany—conducted in early March 1994. The Japanese survey was conducted and published by the *Asahi Shimbun* and the overall results by *The New York Times* (see story in the April 2, 1994, edition of the *Times*). Asked the same question, only 2 percent of Americans polled said that Japan was "the biggest threat."

[9]In the survey, Japanese respondents expressed much greater "trust" in the United States than in Russia, however, with "trust" in the United States comparable to the levels of "trust" in Germany and the United Kingdom and a bit higher than that in China.

[10]The regional focus was even more pronounced among Germans, 53 percent of whom said that Western Europe was the strongest candidate, with 13 percent citing China and 19 percent Japan.

[11]Thirty-one percent of American respondents—the highest percentage of all the countries surveyed—responded that the United Nations had contributed "a lot" to world peace. In both the United States and Japan, 89 percent said that the United Nations had contributed either "a lot" or "some" to world peace.

[12]For two recent contributions to this growing literature, see Masataka Kosaka, *A Regional Approach to Confidence and Security Building in the Far East* (Tokyo: Research Institute for Peace and Security, January 1994) and Michael Krepon, Dominique M. McCoy, and Matthew C.J. Rudolph, eds., *A Handbook of Confidence-Building Measures for Regional Security* (Washington, D.C.: The Henry L. Stimson Center, September 1993).

[13]For a discussion of the history and current trends in this regard, see Donald Zagoria, "Prospects for Organizing the Pacific," in *The US and Japan in the Changing Environment for Multilateral Organizations* (New York: The Ralph Bunche Institute on the United Nations, 1993).

[14]On a non-governmental level, the United Nations Association of the USA (UNA-USA) organized such a quadrilateral forum on Asian security issues from 1990 to 1993.

[15]For a bullish view of the prospects for this development, see David C. Unger, "Get Ready for ARF," Editorial Notebook, *The New York Times*, April 4, 1994.

| TAKAKO UETA | LAYERS OF SECURITY: REGIONAL ARRANGEMENTS, THE UNITED NATIONS, AND THE JAPAN–U.S. SECURITY TREATY |

This paper aims at examining future Japan-U.S. cooperation in peacekeeping under regional security arrangements. For that purpose, it deals mainly with the Japan-U.S. Security Treaty and the Organization on Security and Cooperation in Europe (OSCE)—until January 1995 known as the Conference on Security and Cooperation in Europe (CSCE)—in which Japan has a special participating status. At the moment, there is little likelihood that Japan might participate in NATO's peacekeeping operations, in the North Atlantic Cooperation Council's (NACC) efforts, or in future peacekeeping exercises under the framework of the Partnership for Peace (PFP), mainly because of Japan's self-restriction on peacekeeping activities.

First, in order to avoid confusion, it is worth quoting the NACC's definition of "peacekeeping," which divides peacekeeping into five categories: conflict prevention, peacemaking, peacekeeping, peace enforcement, and peace building. This definition was submitted in the "Report to Ministers by the NACC Ad Hoc Group on Cooperation in Peacekeeping." The report was adopted on the occasion of the meeting of the NACC in Athens on June 11, 1993.

Following are excerpts from the report:

### Conflict prevention

Conflict Prevention includes different activities, in particular those presented under Chapter VI of the U.N. Charter, ranging from diplomatic initiatives to the preventive deployment of troops intended to prevent disputes from escalating into armed conflicts or from spreading.

### Peacemaking

Peacemaking consists of diplomatic actions conducted after the commencement of a conflict, with the aim of establishing a peaceful settlement.

### Peacekeeping

Peacekeeping, narrowly defined, is the containment, moderation, and/or termination of hostilities between or within states, through the medium of an impartial third party intervention, organized and directed internationally, using military forces and civilians to complement the political process of conflict resolution and to restore and maintain peace.

### Peace enforcement

Peace enforcement is defined under Chapter VII of the U.N. Charter as using military means to restore peace in an area of conflict.

### Peace building

Peace building is post-conflict action to identify and support structures that will tend to strengthen and solidify a political settlement in order to avoid a return to conflict. It includes mechanisms to identify and support structures that will tend to consolidate peace, advance a sense of confidence and well-being, and support economic reconstruction and may require military as well as civilian involvement.[1]

Second, it is necessary to summarize the recent developments in U.N. peace efforts and regional security arrangements. U.N. Secretary-General Boutros Boutros-Ghalis's *An Agenda for Peace*, published in 1992, made this point clear: "Under the Charter, the Security Council has and will continue to have primary responsibility for maintaining international peace and security, but regional action as a matter of decentralization, delegation and cooperation with United Nations efforts could not only lighten the burden of the Council but also contribute to a deeper sense of participation, consensus and democratization in international affairs."[2]

*An Agenda for Peace* finds that "regional arrangements or agencies in many cases possess a potential that should be utilized in serving the functions covered in this report: preventive diplomacy, peacekeeping, peacemaking and post-conflict peace-building."[3] *An Agenda for Peace* encourages regional arrangements to contribute to U.N. peace efforts.

After the end of the East-West confrontation, certain regional groupings in Europe that were designed for the Cold War have tried to transform themselves and have taken on new missions. In this context, peacekeeping is one of their new missions since, in the CSCE area, a number of regional conflicts have broken out, and there are many potential conflicts. In particular, the Yugoslavian crisis accelerated this process and has developed the link between the United Nations and regional arrangements such as NATO. The next section outlines the widely defined peacekeeping missions of transatlantic and European regional arrangements that are the focus of this paper.

## PEACEKEEPING BY TRANS-ATLANTIC AND EUROPEAN REGIONAL ARRANGEMENTS

### FRAMEWORK

NATO and the Western European Union (WEU) have adopted new missions of peacekeeping in a wider sense of the word. After the collapse of the Warsaw Pact, NATO sought new missions in order to preserve its collective defense structure. On the occasion of the Rome summit in November 1991, when the NATO heads of state agreed upon the Alliance's "New Strategic Concept," there was no consensus on NATO's role in peacekeeping. At the end of 1991, NATO high officials began to promote the idea of a peacekeeping role. However, French reluctance delayed the process. On June 4, 1992, the NACC ministers met at Oslo and decided to contribute to CSCE peacekeeping. The final communiqué reads as follows: "The Alliance has the capacity to contribute to effective actions by the CSCE in line with its new and increased responsibilities for crisis management and the peaceful settlement of disputes. In this regard, we are prepared to support, on a case-by-case basis in accordance with our own procedures, peacekeeping activities under the responsibility of the CSCE, including by making available Alliance resources and expertise."[4]

The WEU Council on June 19, 1992, issued the Petersberg Declaration, which promised to employ WEU military units for humanitarian and rescue tasks, peacekeeping tasks, and tasks of combat forces in crisis management, including peacemaking.[5]

The CSCE Helsinki summit on July 10, 1992, ruled out the establishment of a CSCE peacekeeping capability and decided to rely instead on existing regional arrangements. However, the summit enhanced CSCE's capability in conflict prevention and crisis management. The OSCE now envisages four stages of intervention. The first stage is "early warning and preventative action." The Committee of Senior Officials (CSO), which is its highest decision-making body, has "primary responsibility." The OSCE Permanent Committee in Vienna has the same responsibility because it meets every week, while the CSO assembles every three months.

The OSCE High Commissioner on National Minorities was established in order to "provide 'early warning' and . . . 'early action' at the earliest possible stage in regard to tensions involving national minority issues."[6] The OSCE has other mechanisms for early warning and early action in the first stage of intervention, such as the Moscow Human Dimension Mechanism and the Valletta Mechanism for Dispute Settlement. The second stage is "Political Crisis Management," in which the CSO takes initiatives in order to relieve tensions. The third stage is the establishment of a framework for negotiating settlements, dispatching rapporteurs, or initiating fact-finding missions. The fourth stage is peacekeeping, which will involve civilian and/or military personnel and may range from observe-and-monitor missions to larger deployments of force. OSCE peacekeeping excludes enforcement action.

In December 1992, NATO enlarged its peacekeeping mandate to include U.N. operations. The final communiqué of the NACC ministerial meeting of December 17 reads as follows: "We confirm today the preparedness of our Alliance to support, on a case-by-case basis and in accordance with our own procedures, peacekeeping operations under the authority of the UN Security Council, which has the primary responsibility for international peace and security. We are ready to respond positively to initiatives that the UN Secretary-General might take to seek Alliance assistance in the implementation of UN Security Council Resolutions."[7]

On December 18, 1992, the NACC foreign ministers issued a statement in which they declared that they are "ready to support and contribute on a case-by-case basis to peacekeeping operations under UN authority or CSCE responsibility, which ensure international legitimacy for such operations."[8] In the "1993 Work Plan for Dialogue, Partnership and Cooperation," which was issued on the same day, consultations on peacekeeping were included for the first time. These covered brainstorming meetings, "joint sessions on planning and peacekeeping missions," "joint participation in peacekeeping training," and "consideration of possible joint peacekeeping exercises."[9] NACC established an Ad Hoc Group on Cooperation in Peacekeeping and adopted three reports on June 11, 1993, in Athens, on December 3, 1993, in Brussels, and on June 10, 1994, in Istanbul. The NACC member countries organized a number of seminars on peacekeeping. Finland, Sweden, Austria, and Ireland are observers at this Ad Hoc Group. The Political-Military Steering Committee of the PFP was merged with the NACC Ad Hoc Group.

For former Warsaw Pact countries that are eager to be NATO members, peacekeeping exercises with NATO members are a politically safe way to enhance interoperability, which they believe brings them closer to NATO. In substance, peacekeeping exercises are nothing but military exercises.

On the occasion of the NATO summit in January 1994, NATO countries adopted the PFP proposal. This proposal offers various forms of cooperation on a bilateral basis, with NATO on the one hand, and with NACC and OSCE countries on the other. PFP is a formula designed for "differentiated cooperation," which was requested by certain countries (those that were not satisfied with the NACC formula). In the Framework Document of the PFP, one objective on peacekeeping is as follows: "The development of cooperative military relations with NATO, for the purpose of joint planning, training, and exercises in order to strengthen their ability to undertake missions in the fields of peacekeeping, search and rescue, humanitarian operations, and others as may subsequently be agreed."[10] In autumn 1994, NATO organized three peacekeeping exercises under the framework of PFP/NACC. A number of peacekeeping exercises have been practiced and planned among NATO member countries and the former Warsaw Pact countries on a bilateral or multilateral basis.

That the NATO and former Warsaw Pact countries are training in peacekeeping is not only reassuring for the latter, namely future NATO members, but will also help to relieve the shortage of peacekeepers. In the future, the United Nations will be more careful in establishing peacekeeping operations; however, in Europe, the OSCE and other organizations will continue to dispatch peacekeepers for their own region.

## PEACEKEEPING OPERATIONS IN PRACTICE

Before establishing its formal framework, NATO gradually began to be involved in the U.N. peacekeeping operations in Yugoslavia. On July 10, 1992, the special NACC ministerial meeting in Helsinki dispatched NATO naval forces to the Adriatic for the purpose of monitoring the U.N. embargo against Serbia and Montenegro. On the same day, before the NATO decision, the special WEU Council agreed to send WEU naval forces to the Adriatic for the same purpose. On June 8, 1993, a single command for the NATO/WEU operation was established.

A high-ranking NATO official analyzed NATO's involvement in peacekeeping from three different perspectives. First, there are three types of participation: contribution of alliance assets to a U.N. or OSCE peacekeeping operation; conduct or coordination of a peacekeeping operation on behalf of either organization; and support for the involvement of individual allies. Second, from the viewpoint of the spectrum of peacekeeping activities, NATO monitors ceasefires and force withdrawals; supervises disarmament and control of weapons; escorts, controls, and protects convoys; creates safe corridors; creates and monitors buffer zones; provides logistical assistance; and removes hazardous munitions. Third, there are three types of alliance contributions: "non-material resources," including information, expertise, techniques, education, training, and coordination; "material resources," including NATO infrastructure, transportation, telecommunications, and logistic support; and "constituted military forces," including NATO collective forces (Standing Naval Force, Atlantic and Standing Naval Force, Mediterranean), elements of the Rapid Reaction Force, the NATO AWACS, and forces from individual NATO countries.[11]

In accordance with U.N. Security Council Resolution 820, NATO engages in enforcement operations of the total embargo against Serbia and Montenegro. Besides Adriatic operations, eight countries initially pledged to send 6,000 troops in order to reinforce the protection of humanitarian transportation operations in Bosnia-Herzegovina. NATO also contributed to the command structure at the U.N. Protection Force II headquarters in Bosnia-Herzegovina to which NATO sent approximately 75 officers from the NATO North (European) Army Group headquarters. NATO contributed AWACS planes for the purpose of monitoring the no-fly zone over Bosnia-Herzegovina, which had been established by U.N. Security Council Resolution 781. Since April 1993, NATO has engaged in "Operation Deny Flight," which is an enforcement of the no-fly zone and U.N. Security Council Resolution 816, which authorized the use of force. In February 1994, NATO fighters shot down violating planes. In May 1993, the U.N. Security Council created "safe areas," and in June, Resolution 836 extended UNPROFOR's mandate to enable the protection of the safe areas. The resolution also authorized member states to use airpower to assist UNPROFOR in carrying out its mandate. Since July 1993, NATO has provided airpower on the basis of this resolution. In August 1993, NACC approved the Military Committee's report, "Operational Options for Air Strikes in Bosnia-Herzegovina." It is the U.N. Secretary-General who authorizes the first use of airpower.[12]

WEU is engaging in the above-mentioned Adriatic operation and in police and customs operations on the Danube for the implementation of the embargo in accordance with the Security Council resolutions.

The OSCE, which defines itself as a regional arrangement under Chapter VIII of the U.N. Charter, attaches importance to preventive diplomacy. The most successful example is the work of Max van der Stoel, High Commissioner for National Minorities, who succeeded in diminishing tensions in Estonia and Russo-Estonian relations that were caused by the alien law in June 1993.[13] He is involved in various minority problems, including that of the Hungarian minority in Slovakia.

The OSCE has sent various missions, including missions that were organized by the Moscow Human Dimension Mechanism, for the purpose of human rights investigations. With regard to Yugoslavia, the OSCE sent three long-duration missions to Kosovo, Vojvodina, and Sandjak, and the Spillover Mission to Skopie in September 1992 in order to prevent conflicts from spreading. The three long-duration missions withdrew because the Belgrade authority refused to prolong their stay. The OSCE has sent missions to Georgia, Estonia, Moldova, Latvia, and Tajikistan for the purpose of helping settle disputes.[14] The OSCE has promoted the Minsk Peace Process on Nagorno-Karabakh and is preparing peacekeeping operations to be implemented after the concerned parties reach agreement.

The OSCE and the European Union (EU) have been jointly engaged in the implementation of the economic sanctions against Serbia and Montenegro. Customs officers were sent to Albania, Bulgaria, Croatia, Hungary, Rumania, Ukraine, and the former Yugoslav Republic of Macedonia.[15]

Finally, it is necessary to refer to the relations between these regional institutions and the United Nations. The U.N. Security Council is the organ that legitimizes the peacekeeping operations of these institutions. The OSCE has two roles: It gives legitimacy to NATO, and it can send peacekeepers itself.

When the European security organizations were established, there was no practical institutional link or cooperation between the United Nations and these organs. Engaging in the Yugoslav operations, both needed to create coordination and cooperation. Between the United Nations and NATO, as well as between the United Nations and OSCE, these practical relations are developing.

During the preparation stage of the CSCE Budapest Review Conference in 1994, Germany and the Netherlands presented a joint proposal that suggested that the CSCE should be primarily responsible for regional disputes in the CSCE region before bringing them to the United Nations. When CSCE efforts are frustrated, the CSCE could refer the dispute to the U.N. Security Council. This idea enjoyed support by the EU member countries and other participants.

## THE JAPAN–U.S. SECURITY TREATY

The Japan-U.S. Security Treaty is not designed for peacekeeping operations, as it has no provision for peacekeeping. In contrast with NATO, there seems to be less of a rationale to add a peacekeeping mission to the Japan-U.S. military alliance in order to prolong its life. The Cold War in Europe ended with the dissolution of the Warsaw Pact Organization and the Soviet Union. The security risk in Europe comes mainly from regional ethnic conflicts and instability in Russia. NATO has to cope with regional conflicts. In Asia and the Pacific, there has been no clear-cut, East-West military confrontation. China is an independent player, and it is difficult to define a common danger in this region. The Japan-U.S. Security Treaty was not designed purely for the Cold War. It has provided security for Japan, which has no full-scale military capability under its present Constitution. The Japan-U.S. Security Treaty itself is not a framework for peacekeeping, but the alliance relations between Japan and the United States are the basis for cooperation in peacekeeping.

With regard to U.N. peacekeeping operations, Japan and the U.S. each have their own policies. The Self-Defense Forces (SDF) have no combat missions, and there are five conditions that must be satisfied before Japanese contingents from the SDF can be dispatched: 1) a ceasefire must be in place; 2) the parties to the conflict must have given their consent to the operation; 3) the activities must be conducted in a strictly impartial manner; 4) participation can be suspended or terminated if any of the above conditions is not met; and 5) participants may not use weapons except in self-defense *stricto sensu,* i.e., in cases where a member of the Japanese contingent is personally attacked.

The United States has taken a reserved approach. In his address to the United Nations on September 27, 1993, President Clinton enumerated four questions that the United Nations must address before undertaking a new mission: 1) Is there a real threat to international peace? 2) Does the proposed mission have clear objectives? 3) Can an endpoint to U.N. participation be identified? 4) How much will the mission cost?[16]

In addition to this, the January 1994 *Report of the Secretary of Defense to the President and the Congress* posited seven questions regarding U.S. participation: 1) Is the use of force necessary at this point? Have other means, including diplomacy, been fully considered? 2) Is the commitment of U.S. forces necessary for the success of the proposed peace operations or to persuade others to participate? 3) Are the stakes or interests involved worth the risk to American military personnel? 4) Will there be domestic political and congressional support for U.S. participation? 5) Has an endpoint for U.S. participation been identified? 6) Are the command and control arrangements for American forces acceptable? 7) In instances involving the significant use of American forces, is the United States committing sufficient forces to achieve decisively its political and military objectives?[17]

On May 5, 1994, President Clinton signed Presidential Decision Directive 25, which defines a comprehensive U.S. policy on multilateral peace operations. The United States will "use peacekeeping selectively and more effectively" because "properly conceived and well-executed peacekeeping can be a very important and useful tool of American foreign policy." The United States will reduce the cost of peacekeeping, which means the reduction of the costs both to the United States and the United Nations. The directive states the belief that the United States has to improve the U.N.'s peacekeeping abilities.[18]

From now on it seems that the United Nations will send fewer peacekeeping forces, and the United States will participate in fewer operations. Japan continues to have a limited role in peacekeeping. Under these conditions, it is not easy to present models of Japanese–U.S. cooperation on peacekeeping.

There have never been joint Japanese-U.S. training or exercises in peacekeeping. Exercises that are limited to logistical support are not significant.

It has been proposed that the United States could help to airlift Japanese peacekeepers and facilities. However, under the U.N. system, Japan cannot delegate a country to perform this function. Another possibility may be humanitarian assistance or disaster operations that are not in the framework of U.N. peacekeeping missions. The SDF have a wealth of experience in disaster operations.

Still another possibility may be to use military facilities and assets in Japan including U.S. bases for U.N. and other peacekeeping missions if necessary.

## THE OSCE AND OTHER EUROPEAN INSTITUTIONS

Japan obtained a special participating formula in July 1992 on the occasion of the CSCE Helsinki Summit.[19] Japan can participate in major OSCE meetings and can contribute to them without participating in its decision-making. As Japan is surrounded by the OSCE region of influence, from San Francisco to Vladivostok, it is necessary that Japan be involved in the process in order to defend its vital security interests.

With Japan's constiutionally imposed restrictions on peacekeeping, the OSCE seems to be a more suitable forum than NATO because its activities are focused on preventive diplomacy without military operations, as was mentioned above, and in the case of peacekeeping, an enforcement mission is excluded.

Japan sent Serbian-language experts to the mission in Vojvodina and has decided to send a Bulgarian-language expert to the Scopie mission. In the future, Japan may contribute civilian missions and logistical support to OSCE peacekeeping. In the framework of the OSCE, Japan and the United States will be able to establish further cooperation.

Lastly, Japan and the United States each have an institutional framework for dialogue and cooperation with the EU and its member states. Within these frameworks, Japan and the United States have committed themselves to reinforcing the United Nations and other international organizations in order to promote security. As most of the members of the EU are American military allies, trilateral cooperation on peacekeeping under the United Nations and the OSCE will be worth considering.

In the case of peace building in Yugoslavia after the real ceasefire, this trilateral cooperation will be effective because the EU will be a major player in the process, and NATO and WEU are expected to contribute to it.

## LOOKING AHEAD

If Japan and the United States participate in the same U.N. peace-keeping operations, the two countries will be able to cooperate closely because of their military alliance. It may be easy for Japan to work with U.S. allies in Europe; however, a Japan-NATO joint operation is unlikely. Despite its present self-restrictions, it might be useful for Japan to attend peacekeeping seminars and courses that are organized by NATO and NACC. It is likely that the peace-keeping modalities, procedures, and future practices in the frame-work of the NACC will influence OSCE and U.N. peacekeeping, because thirty-eight NACC countries and Finland, Sweden, and Austria are participating in the NACC efforts. Finland and Sweden signed the framework document of the PFP in order to participate in peacekeeping activities.

As was mentioned above, Japan may have a role to play in the preventive diplomacy and crisis management functions of the OSCE. In this framework, Japan and the United States, and its European allies can cooperate easily. These countries have a certain amount of interoperability and will be able to engage in humanitar-ian assistance and disaster operations effectively. In the long run, the PFP and the NACC countries will have a certain degree of interoperability.

In Asia and the Pacific, there is no regional security institution that has executed peacekeeping. It is unlikely that the Association of South-East Asian Nations Regional Forum will be equipped for peacekeeping in the near future. It will play a role comparable with the first stage of NACC intervention, described earlier. Like NACC, it will develop a security dialogue including confidence-, security-, or trust-building measures in order to enhance military transparency. It is, after all, the first multilateral security forum in this region, and member countries' security interests are diversified.

In this region, it will be the United Nations that will dispatch peacekeepers. In case of a conflict on the Korean peninsula, the U.N. Security Council will be the source of legitimacy for any operations. In this case, the military assets and resources of the

Japan-U.S. Security Treaty should be utilized due to geographical proximity. The nuclear development of North Korea is not a strictly sub-regional matter, but an issue of proliferation and global concern.

At the moment, the Asia-Pacific Economic Cooperation forum exists solely for the purpose of promoting economic cooperation. This economic cooperation will enhance security in the region.

Costly peacekeeping follows closely on the heels of military conflict. Japan and the United States need to engage in preventive diplomacy beforehand. Both economic giants will be able to stabilize danger by way of development and humanitarian aid, because economic and social difficulties are major causes of conflicts. In this regard, one of the significant activities of the United Nations is development and humanitarian assistance, and this is the right direction for world peace.

United Nations members are trying to reform its institutions. In this process, Japan and the United States should cooperate to make U.N. efforts more efficient and cost effective.

## NOTES

[1]"Report to Ministers by the NACC Ad Hoc Group on Cooperation in Peacekeeping," Meeting of the North Atlantic Cooperation Council, Athens, Greece, June 11, 1993.

[2]Boutros Boutros-Ghali, *An Agenda for Peace: Preventive Diplomacy, Peacemaking and Peace-keeping*, (Report of the Secretary-General pursuant to the statement adopted by the Summit Meeting of the Security Council on January 31, 1992), New York, 1992, p. 37.

[3]Ibid.

[4]"Final Communiqué, 4 June 1992," Ministerial Meeting of the North Atlantic Cooperation Council in Oslo.

[5]"Petersberg Declaration," Western European Union Council of Ministers, Bonn, June 19, 1992.

[6]"CSCE Helsinki Document 1992: The Challenges of Change," Helsinki, July 10, 1992.

[7]"Final Communiqué, 17 December 1992," Ministerial Meeting of the North Atlantic Cooperation Council in Brussels.

[8]"Statement Issued at the Meeting of the North Atlantic Cooperation Council, 18 December 1992," in Brussels.

[9]"Work Plan for Dialogue, Partnership and Cooperation 1993," issued at the meeting of the North Atlantic Cooperation Council held at NATO headquarters, Brussels, on December 18, 1992.

[10]"Partnership for Peace: Framework Document," issued by the heads of state and government participating in the meeting of the North Atlantic Cooperation Council held at NATO headquarters, Brussels, on January 10–11, 1994.

[11]John Kriendler, "NATO's Changing Role—Opportunities and Constraints for Peacekeeping," NATO Review, June 1993, p. 18.

[12]See NAA Defence and Security Committee, "Co-operation in Peacekeeping and Peace Enforcement," Oct. 1993.

[13]See K. Huber, "Averting Inter-Ethic Conflict," Occasional Paper, Carter Center of Emory Univ., 1994.

[14]"Survey of CSCE Long Term Missions and Sanctions Assistance Missions," CPC Secretariat, March 1994.

[15]Ibid.

[16]Address by the President of the United States of America, William J. Clinton, to the 48th Session of the United Nations General Assembly, Sept. 27, 1993.

[17]Les Aspin, Secretary of Defense, Annual Report to the President and the Congress, Jan. 1994, pp. 65-66.

[18]Transcript of the White House Briefing, Policy on Multilateral Peacekeeping Operations, Anthony Lake and Lt. General Wesley Clark, May 5, 1994.

[19]Takako Ueta, "Japan and the CSCE," Michael R. Lucas, ed., The CSCE in the 1990s: Constructing European Security and Cooperation, Nomos Verlagsgesellschaft, Baden-Baden, 1993, pp. 207–22.

WILLIAM J.
DURCH

# 4

MASASHI
NISHIHARA

# JAPAN–U.S. COOPERATION IN U.N. PEACE EFFORTS

The United States and Japan share the luxury of being able to keep most traditional military threats at a distance. With the demise of the Soviet Union and the ongoing conversion of China to a market economy, only North Korean nuclear developments and the possible rise of ultra-nationalism in Russia have the potential to pose a direct military threat to Japan. The United States faces even fewer direct threats. Both have long isolationist episodes in their histories, and this combination of history and geography seems to support continuing hopes in both countries that their international involvement can be limited to low-risk activities without at the same time undermining the positions of world leadership that they either hope to maintain or aspire to, particularly in the United Nations.[1]

However, new, more diffuse challenges to international peace and stability, challenges that can rise to the level of serious security threats if left to grow and spread, are in evidence—from political repression to the rise of ethnic conflict, poverty, pollution, and overpopulation. The foreign policy question for both Washington and Tokyo is how to define national interests so as to meet these new international challenges effectively; this entails convincing their respective domestic public opinion leaders that national interests are indeed at stake. If the United Nations is to be used as the common vehicle for meeting these challenges, it must be seen as an effective institution, or at least as one with sufficient potential that a sustained effort at reform would be worthwhile.

The first part of this paper looks at the question of national interests after the Cold War. The second part discusses concrete cooperative measures that Japan and the United States might support to make the United Nations more effective at conducting peace operations.

## INTERNATIONAL PEACE AND NATIONAL INTERESTS

The U.S. government spent more than a year crafting guidelines to support its decisions to vote for or to participate in U.N. field missions. However, it has addressed the national interests that support such decisions only intermittently, primarily when crises loomed.[2] The lack of sustained attention on the part of the President, the corresponding lack of sustained and coherent public education about America's foreign policy interests, and the natural skepticism of the public and Congress about foreign entanglements have constrained the U.S. government's ability to support, pay for, and participate in U.N. operations. The Clinton Administration's efforts to reframe U.S. interests and foreign policy to encompass such operations have been derailed time and again by ugly real-world events. Its decisions to intervene in places like Bosnia and Rwanda were influenced by such second-order considerations as the quality and intensity of television coverage, the instantaneous emotional responses of voters, and the lobbying efforts of relief agencies.

When the United States engages militarily in potentially risky, quasi-enforcement operations on such bases, as it did in Somalia, Americans' can-do, problem-solving attitude leads many to ignore the inconveniently complex problems underlying a conflict or to believe that they should be fixable in short order, and they fear involvements that may imply a longer-term commitment. The United States is certainly capable of such commitments where its core interests are engaged, as is demonstrated by its defense alliances with NATO and Japan. But such interests must be redefined in terms of the new threats plaguing international stability and human progress if the American people are to understand and support long-term commitments of economic, political, or military resources to contain these threats.

Where interests are not clear, one major casualty-producing event in the course of an operation can lead a country to look for the exit. Knowledge of that tendency—gleaned easily from press coverage of previous conflicts and interventions—may encourage recalcitrant local factions to cause such events. That is, a country that is acutely sensitive to casualties can invite them by making its forces the weak link in the peacekeeping chain. For example, in Rwanda in April 1994, government militias targeted Belgian peacekeepers of the U.N. Assistance Mission for Rwanda (UNAMIR), killing eleven. The Belgian contingent withdrew immediately, taking along with it UNAMIR's communications and logistics capacity and curtailing whatever steps U.N. forces might have taken to stem the subsequent, politically motivated slaughter in that country.[3]

Thus, for the sake of peacekeeping *per se,* and for the safety of its personnel in the field, it is vitally important that a government convince itself that significant national interests are bound up with participation in a U.N. operation, especially one that entails some military risk. It must do so *before* it commits people to the field, lest in the face of adversity it damage its own image, the image of the United Nations, and the integrity of the operation that it has joined.

National security interests are harder to define when the "enemy" is not a consistent and identifiable group of states. In late September 1993, U.S. Ambassador to the United Nations Madeleine Albright defined future threats to U.S. interests in terms of spreading "chaos" in the international system, as exemplified by civil wars and the humanitarian disasters they create, by coups against elected governments, and by gross violations of human rights. According to this analysis, growing disorder could, over time, destroy emerging democratic institutions and open markets in wide swaths of the world, to the lasting detriment of all democracies, even though a given instance of instability might not threaten the vital interests of any major power directly or immediately.[4]

Political leaders trying to deal with these long-term problems face the difficult task of convincing voters and legislators to bear potentially high short-term costs without commensurate short-term payoffs. The case might be easier to make if confronting these problems was thought of as a long-term investment in international stability (based on political pluralism and democracy, market-based economies, and respect for human rights) and as a conflict-containing venture to which many other states contribute. That venture is partly preventive, partly remedial, and occasionally corrective, corresponding to the U.N. terms preventive diplomacy (undertaken to avert conflict); peacemaking (undertaken to negotiate ceasefires and conflict termination); peacekeeping (undertaken to monitor such accords); peace building (to reconstruct shattered polities and economies); and peace enforcement (to suppress conflict or reverse aggression).

## PREVENTIVE DIPLOMACY

Diplomatic initiatives undertaken on the brink of a crisis are not the only preventive measures available to the world community. Longer-term measures, including multilateral technical and financial aid and official development assistance (ODA) from states, can help to avert crises altogether. Japan's four ODA principles, in particular—linking aid to recipients' trends in military spending, democratization, market economics, and environmental protection—can be viewed as crisis preventive insofar as they encourage the evolution of open political and economic systems.[5] Open systems in which there is governmental respect for such basic human and civil rights as freedom from arbitrary arrest, torture, and other capricious and destructive government actions are less likely to harbor aggrieved groups who see force of arms as their only avenue of redress (as in Somalia, Ethiopia, El Salvador, or Chiapas State in Mexico), and thus these systems are more likely to remain stable. The world community, and the industrial democracies in particular, clearly have an interest in preventing such conflicts, and they thus have an interest in influencing the course of events previously thought of as exclusively "domestic," partly because the implosion of several larger Third World states could result in large-scale migration to places where life is better. Western European countries already face waves of refugees from political turmoil, population pressure, and economic decline in North Africa and from conflict in the Balkans. Wholesale collapse in Ukraine or the Russian Federation could produce much larger dislocations presenting would-be host countries with the stark choices of either accepting socially destabilizing numbers of refugees or closing their borders, which could lead to a humanitarian crisis the dimensions of which would dwarf the dramatic Iraqi Kurd exodus of 1991.[6]

As an island nation, Japan is much better positioned than most to resist an influx of displaced peoples, but it depends for its livelihood on overseas economic prosperity and markets, both in the developed and developing world. Dependent on external sources for most of its energy and a significant fraction of foodstuffs, Japan's interest in a stable global economy gives it an abiding interest in overseas political stability and economic development. It has a basic interest in supporting programs and institutions that promote both, and its high levels of ODA attest to that interest.

## PEACEMAKING

When preventive efforts fail and political explosions occur, the world community and its major powers have an interest in seeing that they are contained and that the sources of conflict are addressed and mitigated. Short of direct intervention, however, which is discussed below, the community has little power to alter the behavior of determined combatants who see political value in continued fighting. This has been demonstrated almost daily in Bosnia since April 1992; in Cambodia, where Khmer Rouge resistance in early 1993 came close to derailing the political settlement there; and in Rwanda, where a well-organized, genocidal slaughter erupted despite an internal peace accord and the presence of two thousand U.N. peacekeepers. Nonetheless, where external pressure and internal exhaustion combine to lead local parties to a settlement, outsiders can frequently serve as temporary substitutes for the trust that is always lacking even between former enemies who sincerely wish to end the fighting and let their countrymen get on with their lives.

## PEACEKEEPING

A peacekeeping force is primarily a confidence-building measure whose studiously impartial presence helps to maintain ceasefires between states (for example, on the Golan Heights) and to facilitate implementation of peace accords within states, as in Namibia, El Salvador, Cambodia, and Mozambique. U.N. member states' interests in supporting such operations are well established, historically. Since the publication of U.N. Secretary-General Boutros Boutros-Ghali's *An Agenda for Peace* in mid-1992, the more complex and intrusive of these operations have been dubbed "peace building," which I view as a variation of peacekeeping with more local political involvement and authority. Several of these complex operations have met with reasonable success, while others, in Angola, Somalia, and Bosnia, have been whipsawed by diehard local antagonists. The resources that states are willing to commit at any one time to these ventures are limited, and to some extent peace operations compete with other forms of international aid (e.g., disaster relief, food aid, and ODA) for the same, limited pool of people and funds.[7]

## PEACE ENFORCEMENT

Merely holding one election, even with international help, does not make a country democratic or guarantee that all of its groups and their leaders agree on the futility of violence, which leads to

147

the question of whether the international community should have tools readily available to help emerging democracies face down revanchist threats.[8] Perhaps the forceful overthrow of legitimate democratic governments (as in Haiti and Burundi), or the de facto annulment of free and fair elections (as in Burma [Myanmar], Algeria, Angola, or Nigeria), should result in immediate and automatic external counterpressure, directly from states and regional organizations, and through the United Nations.

Such pressure need not be military in nature at the outset. Targeted economic sanctions, such as freezing telecommunications, capital flows, international air travel, and the foreign assets of coup leaders and their associates, could be a first step. If they were widely understood to be automatic, such measures might deter would-be putschists by promising to sharply constrain their personal access to resources.

Broader economic measures aimed at commodity trade—the more common sorts of economic sanctions—may require military backing to ensure their effectiveness, that is, some combination of naval action and physical control of land routes across the embargoed country's borders. Broad sanctions, however, may do the most damage to the general populace—the very people they are designed to help—while complicit elites retain access to dwindling national resources. Broad sanctions also hurt trading partners, whose commerce with the embargoed state dries up, usually without compensation from the wider community of states.[9]

Whether the international community sees fit to take direct military action in any given case would depend on the specific circumstances of the case. Such circumstances might include, for example,

- the size and location of the country (which would affect operational feasibility);
- the severity of the event (which may range from minor border skirmishes to Iraqi-style invasion; from minor civil strife to anarchy causing widespread starvation; or from selective repression to wholesale genocide); and
- the involvement of more traditional national economic and balance-of-power interests of the would-be intervenors (for example, access to energy sources or to the sea or questions of territorial or political integrity of themselves or allied countries).

The larger the target country, the more remote from the sea, the less acute the event, and the poorer the fit with traditional interests, the less likely will be international military intervention. If action is taken in such cases, the U.N. Security Council may invoke economic sanctions instead of military action (as in the case of South Africa and, more recently, Serbia, Libya, Haiti, and postwar Iraq).

The more accessible the country, the more egregious the action, and the more acute the popular suffering, the more willing the international community may be to entertain direct military measures, all other things being equal. Still, the United Nations is unlikely to move unless a major military power takes the lead (as did the United States in the cases of Kuwait and Somalia and, briefly, in providing relief to Rwandan refugees). Even so, the international community will be inclined to temporize, as it has regarding Bosnia-Herzegovina—a modestly sized, moderately inaccessible place of episodically acute suffering. Such delay occurs even though experience suggests that it raises the price of intervention by giving destructive forces more time to wreak havoc and cause deeper and more widespread mutual hatreds. Delay occurs partly because international institutions other than NATO have no standing capacity to respond militarily and partly because states are operating on the basis of interests keyed to another era.

It is somewhat ironic that the United States chose to lead two U.N.–authorized military interventions on behalf of states (Kuwait and Somalia) that had closed political systems and relatively poor human rights records. On the other hand, the U.N. Charter prohibits aggression against any state, not just states with particular kinds of governments. And based on the arguments just advanced, one might expect non-democratic states to implode more readily than those with open governments, especially since they can no longer count on international support, Cold War style, regardless of how they treat their citizens. Thus the places where the United Nations will be called upon to intervene or to keep the peace will continue to be some of the most difficult places on the face of the earth in which to produce favorable political and military results in reasonable periods of time, and that will always pose problems for decision-makers who need to sell operations to legislatures and the public. Yet those missions may be necessary to prevent even worse outcomes with direct, negative consequences for the industrial democracies.

# U.S.–JAPAN COOPERATION IN IMPROVING U.N. PEACE EFFORTS

As the two largest financial contributors to the U.N. system, Japan and the United States have a special stake in and a special responsibility for that system and a special interest in seeing that it functions more effectively. Areas where they can cooperate to improve its effectiveness include Security Council representation, secretariat-wide reform, U.N. operational planning and support capabilities, training for peace operations, and provision of specialized units to U.N. operations.

## THE SECURITY COUNCIL

What the United Nations is being asked to do today in the security field is both much less and much more than its creators anticipated. The Council was designed to authorize and direct collective responses to international aggression, not to function as a crafter of new social contracts. The Trusteeship Council was designed to guide colonies toward independence, not to take failed states into receivership. The secretariat was intended to support these and other U.N. committees, not to plan and support the field work of 100,000 troops and civilians. Of course, life never goes as planned.

Security Council resolutions are widely viewed as giving the broadest international legitimacy to actions by U.N. member states, other organizations, and the United Nations itself. However, the Council's 1945-vintage structure, updated only slightly with the addition of four members in the early 1960s, no longer adequately reflects the balance of power and interests in the world. The perceived legitimacy of Council decisions, and the willingness of the General Assembly to pay for those decisions, are thus in danger of eroding over time; this has prompted a wide variety of proposals for change. Both Japan and Germany, as major contributors to the United Nations (second and third, financially), would like permanent seats on the Council. The United States supports their membership and recently proposed an expansion of the Security Council to twenty seats.

Any such changes require amendment of the U.N. Charter, however, and must be squared with the demands of larger developing countries that also seek permanent representation.[10] Those demands seem based upon a concept of the Security Council as a geographically balanced conclave of the most populous states with smaller states taking their turn at the table. The veto system, on the other hand, is based on a concept of a Security Council built around the world's most militarily powerful states: originally the victors of World War II, then the acknowledged possessors of nuclear weapons. A third model would allot permanent seats according to economic power, akin to the weighted voting systems used by the World Bank and some other agencies in the U.N. system. The economic-status model underlies the arguments of Germany and Japan for permanent seats.

These differing images of the Security Council cannot easily be reconciled unless developing states can themselves be reconciled to the fact that countries that foot the bills and own the forces want a consistent voice in Council decisions. But perhaps the logic should be carried one step further. Perhaps Council membership (for non-permanent members) and the right to cast a vote on resolutions authorizing field operations should be contingent upon a country's willingness not only to pay its assessments in full and on time but to actively support the peace operations that the Council creates. That is, those with the power to create obligations should have the responsibility to shoulder them as well, in rough proportion to their respective operational capacities. If Charter reform were to make that a criterion for Security Council membership (Article 19 being modified to affect voting in the various Councils of the United Nations as well as the General Assembly), most countries might find periodic membership preferable to a permanent seat (although Article 23 might be modified to permit successive periods of membership with regional caucus endorsement). The Council also might be more careful in the resolutions that it passes and the operations that it authorizes. (To account for the limited ability of smaller Council members representing poorer regions to make in-kind contributions, the in-kind contributions of these members might instead be a regional response.) If the Security Council were revamped along these lines, peace operations would no longer be something that one group of states decides would be good for another group of states to volunteer to do.

Under this concept, Council members' marginal costs to support and participate in the military components of U.N. field operations probably should be borne by them without direct reimbursement from the United Nations, thereby reducing the mission costs that are assessed against the rest of the U.N. membership.[11] If, however, a Council member's contributions to a peace operation (including the value of "in-kind," or non-monetary contributions) exceed the value of that member's normally assessed share of U.N. costs, that excess could be credited by the United Nations against the member's future peace operation assessments, thus allowing Council members to contribute more to some operations that may be particularly important to them, and less to others, "drawing" on their credit to do so.[12]

## SECRETARIAT-WIDE REFORM

Over four decades, the secretariat has evolved into a conservative organization with an administration that is a mix of complex rules and personal influence. Every bureaucracy has a formal and informal organization chart, the former reflecting how things are set up to work and the latter how they actually do work. In the case of the secretariat, the informal structure is strong, in part because many secretariat professional staffers have been in the system for decades and know it intimately, and in part because the formal personnel management system is dysfunctional. At present, the secretariat uses an evaluation system in which 90 percent of the staff receives a top rating.[13] Although anecdotal evidence of "deadwood" abounds, without a useful evaluation system there is no objective basis for pruning. To improve the efficiency of the secretariat, and to make room for new faces in a bureaucracy experiencing little overall growth, Japan and the United States should support the development of an effective personnel management system; greater opportunities for staff training and career development, which will facilitate lateral movement of personnel as technical and operational demands on the organization change; and a system of early retirement with a fixed (perhaps three-year) window of opportunity, opening in 1995, that would offer substantial, one-time separation benefits.

The present secretariat also reflects decades-long efforts by U.N. member states to protect their national interests by insisting on formal shares of professional staff slots; by seeding the system with the "right," government-screened people; or by supplementing their nationals' salaries (in violation of Charter principles) as an incentive for those people to remain in U.N. service. As long as these practices continue, the secretariat will never share the apolitical nature of the best national civil services, because it will not have been able to hire and retain people outside the context of nationalist politics. The United States and Japan should take the lead in promoting the non-political recruitment, retention, and promotion of secretariat staff by supporting a system of entrance exams that apply to all new hires and by encouraging the recruitment of individuals into the U.N. system without the "assistance" of member-state governments. Experienced, senior individuals needed for specific projects or for their specific expertise should be hired on non-renewable short-term contracts or should be borrowed from governments on short-term secondment.

At present, the U.N. personnel system does not reward headquarters personnel who agree to serve in U.N. field missions. Family separation is a problem; few operations have accommodations for spouses, and member states would complain if they provided such accommodations. Although the United Nations does have a Field Service, its members are primarily technical or administrative, not substantive, personnel. The current, de facto incentives for professional and general service U.N. personnel to take field assignments are the often-substantial mission subsistence allowance (per diem) paid to staff who serve in the field and respite from the boredom of underemployment in New York or Geneva. Neither of these is a desirable primary motivation for the staffing of complex and politically sensitive field operations. The United States and Japan should support the development of a U.N. personnel policy that encourages professional staff to take field rotations as prerequisites for promotion in relevant specialties; that pre-designates deployable staff so that headquarters managers can anticipate staff departures for field assignments; and that reserves for individuals who complete field assignments a position with pay grade and responsibilities equivalent to the one they left to go out to the field, much as U.S. employers are supposed to do for military reservists who are called to active duty.

## IMPROVING U.N. MANAGEMENT AND SUPPORT CAPACITY

The United Nations has neither the political clout nor the material resources needed to command, control, or support major combat operations, the language of the U.N. Charter notwithstanding, and it is not likely to acquire them in the near future. Indeed, every time that forces have gone into battle with the blessings of the United Nations, they have fought as ad hoc coalitions, including the first time, in World War II. The Charter writers' efforts to formalize and institutionalize that process of coalition formation were thwarted, apparently by the divisions created by the Cold War, but more fundamentally by the enduring nature of the inter-state system and states' unwillingness to relinquish their formal monopoly of the instruments of violence. To the extent that there is debate about improving the United Nations' institutional capacity to support peace functions, it focuses on the secretariat's capacity to support peacekeeping and peace-building missions. Major enforcement operations will continue to require the additional command and management support of a major power or regional alliance.[14]

A number of structural and procedural reforms designed to enhance the efficiency and effectiveness of U.N. peace functions short of enforcement deserve the support of Tokyo and Washington. They include:

- a single annual accounting period, and ideally a unified budget, for all peace operations, to minimize requirements for special appropriations on the part of member states; budgets of new operations would be matched to the U.N. fiscal year at their first mandate renewal;
- "contingency contracting" to enable the United Nations to adopt a variant of "just-in-time" logistics for new operations;
- mission planning templates and standard costing procedures to permit fast and reasonably accurate initial budget estimates to inform Security Council deliberations on new mission mandates;
- adoption of standardized depreciation schedules for reimbursing member states for the equipment that they use in peace operations; and
- development of modular "mission start-up kits" using equipment recycled from completed missions, filled out as necessary with new procurement, and stored and maintained at an expanded U.N. facility at Pisa, Italy, and at a site to be determined in Asia, to facilitate the rapid deployment of new peace operations.[15]

As an important complement to such improved capacity to plan and budget operations, the U.N.'s Department of Peacekeeping Operations (DPKO) should have the authority to directly recruit the people and purchase the goods and services that field operations require, eliminating the need to rely on the central recruiting and purchasing offices within the U.N.'s Department of Administration and Management. The tempos of recent field operations are so much higher than standard U.N. practice that DPKO should be able to provide for the needs of those operations on its own authority. It used to be that peacekeeping operations were no more hectic than the average U.N. office; that is no longer the case, and the system at large must face up to it.

Finally, complex peace operations increasingly incorporate the work of humanitarian relief agencies and organizations. In 1992, the Secretary-General created a new Department of Humanitarian Affairs (DHA), the job of which is to coordinate the activities of the U.N.'s disparate humanitarian agencies and programs, which are accustomed to operating independently and thus resist centralized management. They have far more experience in doing what they do than has DHA, so its main task is difficult, as is a second, related task: improving coordination between these humanitarian programs and U.N. peacemakers and peacekeepers.

While the humanitarian agencies have found themselves working ever more closely with the peacekeepers in recent years, most find the association discomfiting. The instinct of both the U.N.'s humanitarian agencies and of private relief givers is to send relief as and where it is needed. Tying strings to aid (conditionality) runs against the grain. But just as it is often difficult to separate political and military questions in the field, so it is not always possible to keep humanitarian issues separate from political questions. The selective provision of humanitarian or other reconstruction assistance, for example, could be a valuable tool for a U.N. Special Representative who is trying to cajole reluctant local politicians into implementing the agreements that they have signed (Mozambique would be one case, Somalia might have been another, and the Balkans a third). The culture of humanitarian relief makes this difficult to do and makes rational management of an operation with substantial humanitarian elements especially difficult. Japan and the United States should continue to support DHA's coordinating role for U.N. humanitarian functions at the headquarters and operating-agency levels, but they should also support a management shift that gives the Special Representative in charge of a peace operation full authority over all U.N. agency activities and personnel within that mission's geographic area of operations.

## TRAINING FOR PEACEKEEPING

In the area of training for peacekeeping, important reforms worthy of support would include the following:

- U.N. coordination of the development and application of training standards and procedures for military peacekeepers and civilian police personnel;
- the use of national mobile training teams to "train the trainers" in smaller troop contributing states;
- the use of command-post exercises for likely future staff officers of U.N. operations and, eventually, establishment of a U.N. "command and staff college";[16] and
- support for a policy that recruits peacekeepers first from among states and units that have completed U.N.–standard training and that demonstrate competence in applying those standards.

Masashi Nishihara has suggested that Japan consider sponsoring a joint-peacekeeping training center.[17] Such a center could serve as either a staff or field training facility for personnel (military and civilian) from East and Southeast Asian countries headed for service in U.N. operations. It could facilitate joint training of U.S. and Japanese forces in peacekeeping scenarios as part of the two countries' program of joint defense exercises, and it could be co-located with a reserve stockpile of equipment maintained by Japan in cooperation with the United Nations for peacekeeping contingencies in Asia.

## COOPERATION IN PROVIDING SPECIALIZED MILITARY CAPABILITIES

Japan and the United States are both high-technology societies, and their defense forces reflect that fact. Both countries' forces are well organized and good at engineering, transport, communications, logistics, and medical support. It is often suggested that the way around the political difficulties surrounding both countries' dispatch of combat units to U.N. peace operations—command and control sensitivities for the United States and constitutional implications for Japan—is for both to emphasize such support capabilities, as well as airlift and sealift, which are scarce, globally, in a way that infantry forces are not.

Even in traditional peacekeeping, however, infantry units are the ones most likely to experience casualties, whether from accidents or residual hostilities. In operations with greater risk to ground forces (Somalia or the former Yugoslavia, for example) it is especially difficult to justify a division of labor in which poor countries do the patrolling and keep things secure while the rich countries fly in supplies and build roads or schools. The United States may argue that it holds the world's "stability reserves" and that forces potentially needed for high-intensity combat should not be scattered about the world on what amounts to guardpost and convoy duty. Yet international peace operations require, for their long-term sustenance, a politics of shared risk. Powers that expect to lead the institution must be seen as willing to expose their personnel to risks equivalent to those faced by other powers' troops, whatever else the leading countries may do or provide for field operations. France, Britain, Canada, and the Nordic countries understand this.

According to this line of argument, the United States and Japan should both consider deployment of ground units in U.N. operations. The United States will keep ground units in Haiti when the operation there evolves from its initial multinational coalition to a U.N. peacekeeping force. In early September 1994, Japan announced that it would send about 400 troops to Zaire to aid in relief efforts for Rwandan refugees. Given the continued agitation of Rwandan ex-government officials and troops among the refugee population, the officials' resistance to refugee repatriation, and their declared intent to wage war on the new Rwandan government, this deployment may prove to be riskier than deploying within Rwanda itself, or into areas of Croatia that have been relatively stable for some time. Deployment of an engineering unit in Croatia would undoubtedly gain for Japan considerable standing among the countries of Europe, and it would respond to U.N. Special Representative Yasushi Akashi's appeal for additional troops to support an evolving "peace in parts."[18]

Japan's willingness to send troops to support Rwandan relief efforts should bolster its chances for a permanent seat on the U.N. Security Council, unless those troops face a hostile situation. Under a current provision of the Peacekeeping Operations Law, the defensive use of arms is permitted, in extremis, only on behalf of Japanese personnel. Arguably designed to save lives, this stricture could, in practice, be devastating to Japan's image if it forced Japanese troops to watch without responding while relief workers or their peace-keeping colleagues from other countries were injured or killed by hostile elements.

Recent developments suggest that Japan will continue to be more visible in U.N. operations. On August 12, 1994, a high-level defense advisory panel (the *Bohei Mondai Kondankai*) endorsed, among other things, the overseas deployment of Japanese self-defense units under U.N. command and the amending of current laws to facilitate such participation. Moreover, the Social Democratic Party has finally recognized the constitutionality of the current armed forces, and even its left wing seems to support the seconding of Japanese military units to peace operations under U.N. command.[19]

The advisory panel also endorsed the acquisition of long-range air transport capability. Currently, the United States, Russia, and Ukraine operate the only fleets of heavy military airlifters in the world, and the latter two have been leasing lift capacity to U.N. operations. (Ukraine inherited some 200 former Soviet IL-76 airlifters upon gaining its independence, as well as the Antonov design bureau, builder of the AN-124 Condor heavy-lift transport.) The United States is struggling to replace its current fleet of aging narrow-bodied C-141 aircraft with wide-bodied C-17s. The new program has had a troubled technical history and has experienced considerable unit cost growth over time, the latest because the U.S. Defense Department has reduced its purchase to 40 units pending final testing and certification. On the other hand, the C-17 has much greater range and payload than a C-130 and can land and take off on marginal runways as short as 1,000 meters, enabling direct deployment of people and equipment to remote areas, whether for peacekeeping or disaster relief. Ukraine's Condor has a lift capacity of 150 tons, equivalent to a U.S. C-5 Galaxy, but would not provide the austere field capability of a C-17. Russia's Ilyushin Aviation Company is rolling out a competitor in 1995, the IL-106, designed to carry 80 tons of cargo, and also has rolled out a longer-range version of its IL-76 narrow-body transport able to carry 52 tons 4,500 kilometers.[20]

Were Japan to acquire long-range airlift capability, it would be able to complement U.S. airlift capabilities, in particular, and operate as a full partner in the deployment of U.N. peace operations globally. If it were to purchase C-17s, it could function on an interoperable basis with the United States. Concerns about the appearance of a prohibited military power projection capability might be reduced by permanently detailing these aircraft to a standing International Peace Cooperation Corps headquarters; by pre-designating them for U.N. callup; by making them available secondarily for domestic and regional disaster relief operations; and by relying on American in-flight refueling capacity for long-range deployments. Seeing Japanese airlifters and associated personnel operating in such constructive fashion both in Asia and elsewhere would build a positive image in the minds of recipients and observers alike regarding Japan's contributions to international peace.

Our two countries face similar dilemmas. We want to lead in a discordant world where small conflicts, not big ones, and both long-term trends and short-term problems eat away at global order. But we do not want to risk casualties in the process of leading. If we wish to lead, then we must sometimes do more than pay for others to do the difficult jobs. Some of these jobs we must shoulder as well, in cooperation with others, but as full members of the team.

## NOTES

[1]Author Yasuhiro Ueki suggests that Japan "still lacks a strong internal driving force for activism in multilateral diplomacy . . . [and] views itself as part of a supporting cast for the international order created and maintained by the United States." ("Japan's UN Diplomacy: Sources of Passivism and Activism," in Gerald L. Curtis, ed., *Japan's Foreign Policy After the Cold War, Coping with Change,* Armonk, NY, and London: M.E. Sharpe, Inc., 1993, p. 368.) The problem for the United States is to maintain its old position of leadership when the Cold War "order" it helped to create seems decreasingly applicable to many emerging regional security problems.

[2]The need for criteria to aid decisions about where and how the United Nations should become involved in peace operations is, of course, widely recognized outside the United States as well. See, for example, the report of the Task Force of Policy Council of the Japan Forum on International Relations, *The Strengthening of the UN Peace Function and Japan's Role* (Tokyo: The Japan Forum on International Relations, Inc., October 1992), p. 16. For a discussion of U.S. interests and U.N. operations, see Hon. Nancy L. Kassebaum, et al., *Peacekeeping and the US National Interest,* Stimson Center Report No. 11 (Washington, D.C.: The Henry L. Stimson Center, February 1994), p. 6.

[3]Statement by the former UNAMIR Force Commander, Major General Romeo Dallaire, cited in *International Documents Review* 5:32 (September 5–9, 1994), pp. 4–5.

[4]U.S. Mission to the United Nations, remarks of Ambassador Madeleine K. Albright to the National War College, National Defense University, Washington, D.C., September 23, 1993. Mimeo, pp. 2–3, 6. Some scholars distinguish between a "contagion effect," in which conflicts spill over state boundaries, and a "demonstration effect," in which the international community's reactions to conflict in one region affect the political calculus of leaders and groups weighing violent action in distant regions. The demonstration effect is widely assumed by Western governments, and during the Cold War was combined with the contagion effect in the "domino theory," but it is as difficult to prove as internal conflicts are for outsiders to deter or to extinguish. [See Kamal S. Shehadi, *Ethnic Self-Determination and the Break-up of States*, Adelphi Paper No. 283 (London: International Institute for Strategic Studies, December 1993), pp. 53–56.] Haitian thugs' threats to create "another Somalia" as a U.S. Navy ship approached Port au Prince with peacekeeping troops in late October 1993 and the subsequent reneging on internationally brokered agreements by Haiti's military rulers might suggest a demonstration effect, coming as they did a few weeks after a deadly firefight in Mogadishu and the announcement of the U.S. withdrawal from Somalia.

[5]The four principles of Japan's "ODA charter" were related by former Prime Minister Yasuhiro Nakasone in his recent address, "Changing Japan and its Role," at Chatham House, London, February 24, 1994. Published as IIPS Opinion Piece No. 202E (Tokyo: Institute for International Policy Studies, March 1994), p. 8.

[6]See, for example, Myron Weiner, "Security, Stability, and International Migration," *International Security* 17:3 (Winter 1992–92), pp. 91–126; Doris Meissner, "Managing Migrations," *Foreign Policy* 86 (Spring 1992), pp. 66–83; James Rupert, "World's Welcome Strained by 20 Million Refugees," *Washington Post*, November 10, 1993, p. A32; and Gil Loescher, *Beyond Charity: International Cooperation and the Global Refugee Crisis* (New York: Oxford University Press, 1993), esp. chapters 5, 7, and 8. Population displacement is not the only, or even the most immediately destructive, byproduct of poverty in developing countries, however. The United States, Europe, and other states face a continuing influx of illegal drugs the raw materials of which are grown largely by peasants who have no better economic alternatives. See Kenneth E. Sharpe, "The Military, the Drug War, and Democracy in Latin America," a paper prepared for the conference on "Warriors in Peacetime," Inter-American Defense College, Washington, D.C., December 11–12, 1992; Salamat Ali, "Opiate of the Frontier: Pakistan's tribes find it hard to give up poppy crop," *Far Eastern Economic Review*, May 27, 1993, p. 18; and William Matthews, "Victory Eludes DOD in Drug War: Pentagon Begins to Shift Tactics in Counternarcotics Effort," *Defense News*, March 28–April 3, 1994, p. 22.

[7]Occasionally, peacekeeping and development efforts converge, as in Cambodia and Mozambique, where most of the money for demobilizing the current army and the Mozambique National Resistance (RENAMO) guerrillas comes from bilateral and multilateral donations and not from the budget of the U.N. Operation in Mozambique (ONUMOZ), the U.N. peacekeeping operation.

[8]Conflicts involving *secession* from central authority are more complex for the international community to deal with than are conflicts involving *competition for control* of central authority. The former involve competing principles of international law that support self-determination but oppose changing borders by force. Examples of secession conflicts include those in Georgia, Nagorno-Karabakh, and the former Yugoslavia.

[9]See Gary Clyde Hufbauer, et al., *Economic Sanctions Reconsidered*, 2nd ed. (Washington, D.C.: Institute for International Economics, 1990), esp. chapters 4 and 5.

[10]*International Documents Review* 5:2, January 24, 1994, pp. 4–5. *Dallas Morning News*, March 23, 1994, p. 16.

[11]Such costs would include the salaries and mission subsistence allowances of U.N. and other civilian international staff, salaries of staff hired within the host country, transportation and housing, and costs related to civil administration, humanitarian relief, police and election oversight, and other non-military elements of the operation. Thus, the larger the military fraction of mission costs, the lower the proportional burden on non-Council members.

[12]This discussion does not address the issue of which scale of assessments should be used to finance future peace operations—the "peacekeeping" scale or the "regular" scale—but the implication of the suggested reforms would be the elimination of the peacekeeping scale, particularly since Security Council members would bear most of the costs of the military components of peace operations.

[13]Peter Fromuth and Ruth Raymond, "UN Personnel Policy Issues," in Peter Fromuth, ed., *A Successor Vision: The United Nations of Tomorrow* (Lanham, Md.: University Press of America, 1988), p. 236. The same statistic also appears in Under-Secretary-General Richard Thornburgh, "Report to the Secretary General of the United Nations," (New York: mimeo, March 1, 1993), p. 10.

[14]For further discussion, see William J. Durch, *The United Nations and Collective Security in the 21st Century* (Carlisle, PA: Strategic Studies Institute, U.S. Army War College, February 1993), esp. pp. 21 ff.

[15]Several of these proposals may be found in the Secretary-General's report on "Effective planning, budgeting and administration of peace-keeping operations," General Assembly document A/48/945, May 25, 1994 (released late July 1994).

[16]For a complete assessment of training requirements and alternative models of U.N. support for training, see Barry M. Blechman and Matthew Vaccaro, *Training for Peacekeeping: The United Nations' Role* (Washington, D.C.: The Henry L. Stimson Center, May 1994).

[17]Masashi Nishihara, "Trilateral Country Roles: Challenges and Opportunities," in John Roper, et al., *Keeping the Peace in the Post-Cold War Era: Strengthening Multilateral Peacekeeping* (New York, Paris, and Tokyo: The Trilateral Commission, 1993), p. 64.

[18]John F. Harris, "Special Envoy Urges US Troops for Balkans," *Washington Post*, March 31, 1994, p. A16. See also "Walking the Extra 1,000 Miles," *Washington Post* editorial, April 1, 1994, favoring U.S. troop contributions.

[19]Naoaki Usui, "Japan May Expand Regional Clout," *Defense News*, August 15–21, 1994, p. 1; Eiichiro Sekigawa, "Panel Urges Overhaul of Japan's Military," *Aviation Week and Space Technology*, August 22, 1994, p. 59; Kensuke Ebata, "Draft proposal edges Japan toward pacifism," *Jane's Defense Weekly*, September 10, 1994, p. 3; and Hiroshi Suzuki, "Japan Seeks clarity on Africa mission," *United Press International* (wire, September 5, 1994, 8:18 am GMT).

[20]Piotr Butowski, "Ilyushin looks to take on Antonov," *Jane's Defence Weekly*, January 23, 1993, p. 22; John Tirpak, "C-17, theater missile defense buys may be in Japan's future," *Aerospace Daily Focus: International Markets*, August 19, 1994, p. 283; and Paul Duffy, "Stretch revives IL-76 prospects," *Flight International*, June 28-July 4, 1995, pp. 45, 48.

| MASASHI NISHIHARA | JAPAN–U.S. COOPERATION IN U.N. PEACE EFFORTS |

## THE RATIONALE FOR JAPAN–U.S. COOPERATION

As the end of the Cold War has broken the recurrent discord that existed among the permanent members of the U.N. Security Council, the role of U.N. peace operations has gained quickly in import as a multilateral means to respond to regional conflicts. Between 1948 and 1993, there were thirty-two U.N. peacekeeping operations, of which as many as fourteen were created after 1991: five in 1991, four in 1992, and five in 1993. Some operations were successful, while others were less so. But the number of U.N. operations is likely to grow in the future.

Among many issues that should be raised to make U.N. operations more effective, an important question may be whether or not U.N. peace operations would be more effective if certain nations would cooperate more closely among themselves. Nordic countries (Denmark, Finland, Norway, and Sweden), for instance, usually send combined forces for U.N. peace efforts, including the U.N. Protection Force in the former Yugoslavia. In September 1992, the U.S. Air Force airlifted 500 Pakistani peacekeepers to Mogadishu. In 1992 and 1993, Japanese transports were used to help transport some of the equipment and other relevant materials of Philippine contingents for U.N. Transitional Authority in Cambodia (UNTAC) activities. Are there any areas where Japan and the United States, two large powers whose gross national products together make up about 40 percent of the world's total, can do similar things?

Japan and the United States began to participate in post–Cold War U.N. peace efforts from contrasting perspectives—with Japan as a self-restrained peacekeeper and the United States as an active peace enforcer. Subsequent damaging experiences that the United States underwent in Somalia in 1993, however, have pushed it back to the status of a cautious participant. The U.S. government has since reviewed its policy on U.N. peace operations and has now come up with a dramatically changed position.[1] The new stand is seriously to question whether individual U.N. operations and U.S. involvement are really warranted. In the words of Anthony

Lake, President Clinton's national security adviser, "Do the UN peace operations always benefit the American people? No."[2] A Presidential Decision Directive issued in May 1994 maintains that "the U.S. and UN involvement in peacekeeping must be selective and more effective."[3]

In the meantime, the dramatic political realignments in Japanese politics that have taken place since July 1993 have culminated in a coalition government composed of the Japan Social Democratic Party (JSDP) (formerly called the Japan Socialist Party), the Liberal Democratic Party, and the small Forerunners. Prime Minister Tomiichi Murayama, who has headed the left-wing group within JSDP, drastically reversed his position in July 1994 and supported the constitutionality of the Self-Defense Forces (SDF) and the importance of the Japan–U.S. Security Treaty. Murayama, who filibustered against passage of the International Peace Cooperation Bill only two years earlier, decided to dispatch some 200 Japanese troops to Zaire in September 1994 by applying that very law.

The new political developments in Japan suggest that it will become more positive about participating in U.N. peace operations. However, the gap between the Japanese and U.S. governments is naturally still wide in that Washington still retains the option to participate in U.N. peace-enforcement operations whereas Tokyo rules out that option. Yet the two positions, which have moved to a common ground, seem to provide a basis for closer bilateral cooperation.

An attempt is made here to explore what the two countries can do together in order to strengthen U.N. peace operations. There are at least two reasons to promote this attempt. First of all, the two countries, which often talk about "global partnership," need some common demonstrable work. The slogan "global partnership" tends to lose its substance when it is overshadowed by the ongoing trade frictions. To work together for a larger goal of international peace and security will strengthen overall political relations between the two countries.

Second, to promote Japanese-American cooperation for U.N. peace efforts, based on the existing security arrangements, will help the two governments justify the *raison d'être* of the alliance before their own people. In the post–Cold War period, faced with the absence of the Soviet threat, the two governments have to explain to their own people why their alliance relations should be continued.

To talk about Japanese-American cooperation in promoting U.N. peace efforts does not mean to, and should not, exclude the participation of other nations. It is important to note at the outset that Japanese-American cooperation in U.N. peace operations should not be undertaken exclusively. U.N. peace efforts do have and should have a multinational character. In Cambodia, UNTAC personnel, composed of 5,000 civilians and 15,000 military personnel, came from some 40 countries. If the two countries alone conduct joint operations as designated under U.N. Security Council resolutions, such operations may be interpreted as efforts to establish "a Japanese-American condominium," to which the Asians would be particularly sensitive. Tokyo and Washington should be careful to avoid creating this impression.

Japan and the United States should work closely with South Korea in supporting U.N. peace efforts in Asia. They should also work with the "regional arrangements," as stipulated in Chapter VIII of the U.N. Charter. Today there are two such regional arrangements in Asia: the Association of South-East Asian Nations (ASEAN) and the Five Power Defense Arrangement (FPDA) (Great Britain, Australia, New Zealand, Singapore, and Malaysia). So far Japan has formal security cooperation with neither ASEAN nor FPDA. The United States is also in almost the same situation, although it has bilateral military exercises with ASEAN member nations and provides military training programs for ASEAN officers in its own country.

## THREE TYPES OF BILATERAL COOPERATION AND CONSTRAINTS

The United States has security treaties with Japan and South Korea. It deploys about 2,000 Army personnel and 22,000 Marines in Japan and 32,000 Navy personnel in Japan and Guam plus 27,000 Air Force personnel in Japan and South Korea.[4] Japanese and American troops often conduct joint exercises. In 1992 and 1993, the two forces had eighteen combined exercises.[5] These experiences offer a solid base for contemplating bilateral cooperation in strengthening U.N. peace efforts as well as in defending Japan and maintaining the security of the Far East.[6] It should be noted that the Japanese–U.S. Security Treaty stipulates that "The Parties will endeavor to concert with other peace-loving countries to strengthen the United Nations so that its mission of maintaining international peace and security may be discharged more effectively" (Article 1).

Bilateral cooperation, if it is to be successful, must assume that the two parties understand each other's policy and legal and political constraints in implementing the cooperative scheme. Each party must also have a close understanding of the other's equipment and peculiarities. Joint or combined training, language training, and the like will be required. There will be primarily three forms of bilateral cooperation: 1) American logistical support of Japanese missions under U.N. operations; 2) Japan's logistical support of U.S. missions under U.N. operations; and 3) Japan–U.S. joint missions on site as designated by the U.N. Security Council and the Secretary-General. Each form presents new opportunities for stronger U.N. peace operations, but each also suffers from varying degrees of obstacles—constitutional, legal, and political—which will be discussed here.

## U.S. LOGISTICAL SUPPORT OF JAPANESE MISSIONS

To promote bilateral cooperation for U.N. causes, the United States can use its power-projection capabilities, based in Japan, and provide airlift and sealift capabilities for Japanese troops when Japan decides to participate in U.N. operations in such remote places as southern Europe (e.g., the former Yugoslavia), the Middle East, and Africa. The largest transports that the Air Self-Defense Forces has are C-130 transports, which can carry only ninety-two persons at a time. The Air Self-Defense Forces has only fifteen of them. They can fly for the distance of 3,700 kilometers (about 2,300 miles) and thus have to stop over at four or five places before they can reach their destinations in Mozambique, which is about 12,000 kilometers away. Large commercial planes such as the B-747 were used during the UNTAC operations. They transported Cambodia-bound Japanese troops to a Thai military airport, from where they were taken by U.N. helicopters to Phnom Penh.

Japanese diesel-powered naval ships also can sail for only a short distance without fuel supply ships, which are also diesel powered. Cambodia-bound ships had to stop over at three places before they arrived in Sihanoukville.

There is no provision in either Japanese or American law that prohibits American assistance in Japanese U.N. missions. In May 1993, a Japanese newspaper reported that the Tokyo government had sounded out the U.S. government about the possibility of the United States providing transportation and food-supply services, if necessary, for Japanese U.N. missions in remote areas.[7] In May 1993, Toshio Nakayama, Minister of State for Defense, expressed his strong desire for U.S. support of Japanese peacekeeping missions in Mozambique in the field of transportation.[8] The government also had the idea of setting up joint training centers within U.S. bases in Japan. None of these possibilities have yet been realized. In the future, the two nations may discuss the possibility of Japanese missions using U.S. bases in Diego Garcia as transit stations.

## JAPAN'S LOGISTICAL SUPPORT OF U.S. MISSIONS

The question of what kind of logistical support Japan can provide for U.S. missions is a large and complicated one. This will involve Japan's constitutional debates and thus political constraints. Primarily two issues are involved: What is the nature of a U.S. mission, and where is it going to be operated?

The nature of U.S. missions can be divided into three categories: a peace-enforcement mission supported by Chapter VII of the U.N. Charter but not organized under U.N. command (the Gulf War–type multinational coalition forces); a peace-enforcement mission led by a U.N. commander under Chapter VII of the Charter (U.N. Operation in Somalia II–type forces); and a peacekeeping mission organized under "Chapter VI½."

According to the current official interpretation of its Constitution, Japan can use force only for self-defense. Article 9 of the Constitution has caused agonizing debates both inside and outside the National Diet ever since its inception in 1947. It stipulates: "Aspiring sincerely to an international peace based on justice and order, the Japanese people forever renounce war as a sovereign right of the nation and the threat or use of force as a means of settling international disputes." Thus when the government introduced an International Peace Cooperation Bill in the spring of 1992, it had to compromise with the opposition parties, who argued that engaging in U.N. peacekeeping operations that may involve "the use of force" is unconstitutional. The bill passed with an important condition, which was to "freeze" participation in military aspects of peacekeeping operations for at least three years. The government's position then was to distinguish between traditional peacekeeping operations that may involve the use of force in self-defense and peace-enforcement operations that may involve the use of force in combat, and to regard the former category of peace efforts as constitutional. However, because of the stern opposition of the opposition parties, the government compromised by restricting Japanese participation to a third category of strictly non-military functions, with a "freeze" placed on the performance of many traditional peacekeeping functions for three years.

Thus Japan cannot be engaged in assisting the first two categories of U.S. missions, while it can take part in the third category of mission to the extent that it does not involve "military activities." The distinction between peacekeeping operations that may involve military activities and those that are free of military activities is important to Japanese lawmakers. Patrolling a ceasefire line, disarming hostile forces, and de-mining are considered military activities and are "frozen," while civic activities such as road construction, bridge repair, and communications and transportation services are permitted.

With regard to the location of Japanese support for U.S. missions, the SDF can render little support, so far as airlift and sealift capabilities are concerned. American forces are self-reliant. The best the Japanese government could do under the circumstances would be to procure sealift and airlift capabilities that the Japanese private sector may possess. Even this option is hard to realize. During the Gulf War, the U.S. government asked Japan whether it could procure commercial planes to help transport American troops and equipment from the continental United States to the Middle East. The government had to decline because the trade unions of Japan Airlines and All Nippon Airways refused to respond positively on the ground of the risky nature of their assignments. The government ended up by procuring some American commercial airplanes to provide the service. Japan needs emergency laws that empower the Prime Minister to procure airlift and sealift capabilities from the private sector. The need to adopt emergency bills was raised in the National Diet several times in the past, but attempts to do so always failed because of the resistance of the opposition parties. However, with the Socialist Prime Minister now accepting Japan's international security role, it has become possible for the major parties to agree on the adoption of new emergency laws.

## JOINT MISSIONS ON SITE

Japan and the United States may find it useful and wise to cooperate in certain U.N. peace operations. As was noted before, all U.N.

peace efforts are essentially of a multinational nature and should not be undertaken by two countries alone. Yet certain U.N. operations may have the two countries' roles at their core.

U.N. peace operations may be placed in three categories in terms of military involvement: non-military or civilian operations (such as repairing roads and monitoring elections), traditional peacekeeping operations (such as patrolling demilitarized zones and de-mining), and peace-enforcement operations. In participating in the first kind of operation, the two countries face few legal and political constraints. However, in undertaking the second and third operations they face different degrees of legal and political obstacles.

Under the current official interpretation of its Constitution, as mentioned earlier, Japan is prohibited from becoming engaged in peacekeeping operations that may involve the use of force. The second and third kind of U.N. peace operations fall under this category. The International Peace Cooperation Law became effective in August 1992; it set out five principles governing Japanese participation in U.N. forces:

1. There must be a ceasefire agreement in place among the parties concerned;

2. There must be consent among the parties concerned regarding Japanese participation;

3. The U.N. presence must be neutral to the parties to the conflict;

4. Japan must maintain its right to withdraw its own contingents in case any of the above three conditions fails to be met; and

5. The situation requires no more than minimum armament for the self-protection of Japanese contingents.[9]

The law defined Japan's role in the way "traditional" peacekeeping operations have been defined. However, it should be remembered that an important condition—effective for at least three years—was attached to this law: Japanese troops should not be engaged in military aspects of traditional peacekeeping operations such as patrolling demilitarized zones (Additional Provisions, Article 2). Japan is "a self-restrained peacekeeper."[10]

In the meantime, the Clinton Administration has reversed its initial activist policy on participation in U.N. peace efforts. The new policy, announced in May 1994, set stricter guidelines for U.S. involvement:

1. Participation must advance U.S. interests;
2. Personnel, funds, and other resources must be available;
3. U.S. participation must be necessary to the operation's success;
4. The role of U.S. forces must be tied to clear objectives;
5. Domestic and Congressional support must either exist or be able to be marshalled; and
6. Command and control arrangements must be acceptable.[11]

Both the Japanese and the U.S. governments want to set limits on their involvement in U.N. peace efforts, although their limits are different. While Japan wants to put legal limits on participation, the United States seeks to place practical limits in terms of cost and benefit. Japan is confined to non-military (civilian) and limited (self-restrained) peacekeeping, whereas the limits imposed by the United States will apply to all peacekeeping. Under these circumstances, restrained Japanese peacekeepers and American peacekeepers will find it difficult to work together well. What is worse, restrained Japanese peacekeepers and American peace enforcers can hardly work together. The latter case is exemplified by the situation in Bosnia today where Nordic, French, and British troops are deployed on the ground as peacekeepers while the U.S. government urges the United Nations and NATO to take tough punitive air strikes against the Bosnian Serbs. Such action is likely to endanger Nordic peacekeepers. The Japanese troops would not be placed in that kind of situation.

The discussion of joint missions on site demonstrates the difficulty of Japanese-American cooperation today. The only area where the two troops can work together is in the field of non-military aspects of peacekeeping operations. If Japan should change its interpretation of its Constitution, Japanese forces can then participate in U.N. peace operations as "full-fledged peacekeepers," which would certainly widen the basis for bilateral cooperation. If the forces of the two countries are to work together in the future, they should begin to study in advance the rules of engagement, the interoperability of communications equipment, and the like. They should also conclude an acquisition and cross-serving agreement to facilitate reciprocal refueling and repairing.

# PROSPECTS FOR BROADER BILATERAL COOPERATION

The current constraints upon Japanese–U.S. cooperation for U.N. peace operations stem from severe constitutional and political conditions placed upon Japanese roles. Prospects for closer bilateral cooperation will be determined first by a change in Japanese policy. But the prospects may also become brighter if there is a willingness by the two governments to work more actively to build regional arrangements, particularly for preventive diplomacy in the Asia-Pacific region.

## PROSPECTS FOR A CHANGE IN JAPANESE POLICY

The current clause in the peacekeeping legislation banning Japan's participation in military aspects of peacekeeping operations can be reviewed beginning in August 1995. If the majority of the Diet members should favor eliminating this ban, can Japan then send troops as full-fledged peacekeepers? The report by the Prime Minister's Advisory Group on Defense Studies recommended in August 1994 that Japan remove this ban as soon as possible.[12] Opponents of the ban point out that conditional participation in U.N. peacekeeping operations will undermine the government's wish to obtain a permanent seat on the U.N. Security Council. Moreover, supporters of the ban may change their view if about 200 Japanese troops stationed in Zaire, and armed with sidearms and only one light machine gun each, should face fatal attack by local, undisciplined Zairean troops or Rwandan refugees.

Changes in Japanese policy toward U.N. peace operations may also be possible if political alignments change. For example, if the New Frontier Party (formed in December 1994 from the former Renewal Party and three smaller opposition parties) should emerge as a leading party, it is likely to take an activist policy on Japanese participation. Ichiro Ozawa, who is a prominent leader in the party, has argued that Japan should establish a U.N. reserve force, distinct from the SDF, "for deployment in response to UN requests and under UN command." He further maintains that the establishment of such a force "would in no way violate the Japanese Constitution."[13] The Japanese public, however, may be slow in responding to such an activist stand, for it is still reluctant to see Japanese troops taking up U.N. missions that involve the use of force.

171

## JOINT EFFORTS IN BUILDING UP REGIONAL ARRANGEMENTS: THE CASE FOR THE SOUTH CHINA SEA

While Japan and the United States face difficulty in finding areas of cooperation for U.N. peace operations *per se*, they should attempt to strengthen diplomatic cooperation in building up regional arrangements. As Chapter VIII of the U.N. Charter provides, the United Nations encourages the role of "regional arrangements or agencies for dealing with such matters relating to the maintenance of international peace and security as are appropriate for regional action, . . . " (Article 52). Faced with financial difficulties in running so many peacekeeping operations, Secretary-General Boutros Boutros-Ghali convened a meeting on August 1, 1994, to which he invited the representatives of over ten regional organizations such as NATO, the Commonwealth of Independent States, and the Organization of African Unity (OAU), urging them to take over the burden of tackling regional conflicts.[14]

The Asia-Pacific region has several potential flashpoints, including relations between North and South Korea, Sino-Taiwan relations, Sino–Hong Kong relations, and conflicting claims over the islands in the South China Sea. China maintains that the Taiwan and Hong Kong issues are its internal issues. However, if armed conflicts should start or should be about to start over these issues, they would quickly assume international dimensions. Japan and the United States should begin to build up regional arrangements to deal with potential regional issues. The region has no organizations equivalent to NATO or OAU. The Manila Pact of 1954 is still valid, but the South-East Asia Treaty Organization, once organized on the basis of the Pact, has been defunct for some time. Nor are there Association of South-East Asian Nations (ASEAN) forces as such, although there was some effort on the part of ASEAN to link itself directly to the United Nations. The ASEAN Regional Forum (ARF), which was started in July 1994, has just begun to consider what it can do to promote mutual trust in the region, and it is not organized to take "regional action," as Article 52 of the U.N. Charter stipulates.

Japan and the United States should jointly study how to handle such regional issues as the disputes over the South China Sea, where six nations compete over territorial claims to the Spratly and Paracel Islands. Indonesia, with Canada's financial help, has been holding annual informal consultative meetings with the claimants on this issue since 1990, but this strategy has so far produced no desirable results.[15] In the meantime, China, Vietnam, and Malaysia are building new military installations on the islands they occupy. Tensions between China and Vietnam are especially acute.

If armed clashes should occur, the U.N. Security Council may not be able to take any action over the veto that China, which is a permanent member, would probably exercise. However, depending on how military tensions develop, China may find it in its interest to see a U.N. naval and air peacekeeping force patrolling the area and observing the movement of naval ships and military aircraft in the South China Sea. China, Vietnam, the Philippines, and Malaysia cannot participate in the U.N. operations, because they are parties to the disputes. Nor can ASEAN and the FPDA serve as neutral, non-partisan forces, for some of the members may be parties to the conflict.

In such a situation, Japan and the United States may be asked to serve as a core force in a U.N. naval peacekeeping force in the South China Sea. The United States will have to provide logistical support for Japanese missions. If China should veto any U.N. action, it may then be wise for Japan and the United States and other like-minded countries to organize a regional peacekeeping force of which Japanese and American forces serve as major components. Such a force may well be deployed in order to prevent the outbreak of armed clashes. Again, a change in Japan's policy toward the use of force is necessary for its full participation.

Such a U.N. naval peacekeeping force or a regional peace-keeping force may well be endorsed by a regional agency, such as the ARF or the ASEAN Post-Ministerial Conference (PMC). The former includes China, whereas the latter does not. Depending on how China will behave, either the ARF or the PMC may be able to support such a force.

## CONCLUSION

Japan and the United States, two major powers that together with many others are responsible for the maintenance of international peace and security, should consider positively how they can work together, in order to promote U.N. peace operations. This will not only help strengthen the bilateral alliance and substantiate the slogan "global partnership" but will also help improve the security of the Asia-Pacific region.

The two countries can contemplate three types of bilateral cooperation: American logistical support for Japanese missions, Japanese logistical support for American missions, and joint missions on site. U.S. airlift and sealift capabilities, based in Japan, can be utilized for the logistical support of Japanese missions, while Japan, lacking in power-projection capabilities, can provide stronger host-nation logistical support for American missions.

Tokyo and Washington have their own policies and conditions for participating in U.N. peace efforts. These policies and conditions are reflections of their constitutional and political constraints. Under the current interpretation of its Constitution, Japan can participate in only those U.N. peacekeeping operations that will *not* involve the use of force. The United States, while having no such legal obstacles, is similarly cautious on deciding to commit its troops to U.N. peace efforts. However, the gap between the two countries is still serious, which makes it difficult for them to seek joint U.N. missions overseas.

The future possibility of closer bilateral cooperation in U.N. peace efforts depends upon changes in Japanese attitudes toward the use of force and the willingness of the two governments to attempt to build up regional arrangements to help settle regional disputes. Their forces, for instance, can serve as the core of a U.N. peacekeeping force or of a regional peacekeeping force to stabilize the tensions in the South China Sea.

If Japan and the United States can work effectively to promote the causes of Chapters VI, VII, and VIII of the U.N. Charter, their relationship will assume a new dimension. The bilateral alliance will then promise to become more solid than before.

## NOTES

[1]Many U.S. reports discussing U.S. participation in U.N. peace-enforcement operations appeared until the summer of 1993, when they seem to have stopped coming out. Some reports favoring a U.S. role in peace-enforcement operations include: Jeffrey I. Sands, *Blue Hulls: Multinational Naval Cooperation and the United Nations*, Alexandria, VA, Center for Naval Analyses, 1993; William J. Doll and Steven Metz, *The Army and Multinational Peace Operations: Problems and Solutions*, Carlisle Barracks, PA, Strategic Studies Institute, U.S. Army War College, and U.S. Peacekeeping Institute, 1993; Edward J. Dennehy, et al., *A Blue Helmet Combat Force*, Cambridge, MA, National Security Program, John F. Kennedy School of Government, Harvard University, 1993; and Naval War College, compiled, *Conference on Options for U.S. Participation in United Nations Sanctioned Military Operations*, Newport, RI, Strategy and Campaign Department, 1993, Research Memorandum, 2–93.

[2]Anthony Lake, ''The Limits of Peacekeeping,'' *The New York Times*, February 6, 1994, Section IV, p. 17.

[3] U.S. Department of State, *The Clinton Administration's Policy on Reforming Multilateral Peace Operations*, Bureau of International Organization Affairs, Department of State Publication 10161, May 1994, p. 1.

[4]Japan Defense Agency, *Defense of Japan 1993* (Tokyo, *The Japan Times*, 1993), pp. 56–57.

[5]Japan Defense Agency, ibid., pp. 247–49.

[6]See Article 6 of the Treaty of Mutual Cooperation and Security between Japan and the United States, which stipulates that ''For the purpose of contributing to the security of Japan and the maintenance of international peace and security in the Far East, the United States of America is granted the use by its land, air and naval forces of facilities and areas in Japan.''

[7]*Yomiuri Shinbun*, May 17, 1993.

[8]Ibid.

[9]Translation is the author's. A similar translation is seen in ibid., p. 128.

[10]Masashi Nishihara, ''Trilateral Country Roles: Challenges and Opportunities,'' in John Roper, et al., *Keeping the Peace in the Post–Cold War Era: Strengthening Multilateral Peacekeeping*, New York, The Trilateral Commission, 1993, pp. 49–66.

[11]U.S. Department of State, op cit., p. 5.

[12]Advisory Group on Defense Studies, *The Modality of the Security and Defense Capability of Japan: The Outlook for the 21st Century*, August 1994, p. 14.

[13]Ichiro Ozawa, *Blueprint for a New Japan: The Rethinking of a Nation* (Tokyo, Kodansha International, 1994), p. 119.

[14]*Sankei Shinbun*, August 13, 1994.

[15]Canadian Consortium on Asia Pacific Security, ''South China Sea Project,'' *CANCAPS Bulletin*, No. 2, May 1994, pp. 3–5.

# ABOUT THE AUTHORS

**Masahiko Asada** is Associate Professor of International Law at Okayama University. A former Visiting Research Fellow at York University and a Senior Associate at St. Antony's College, Oxford, England, he served as Legal Advisor to the Japanese delegation to the Conference on Disarmament in Geneva from 1991 to 1993. He is the co-author of *Superpower Maritime Strategy in the Pacific.*

**William J. Durch** is a Senior Associate of the Henry L. Stimson Center. He has served as assistant director of the Defense and Arms Control Studies Program at the Massachusetts Institute of Technology, has taught at Georgetown University, and has held research positions at MIT, Harvard, and the Center for Naval Analyses. He is co-author of *The Evolution of UN Peacekeeping: Case Studies and Comparative Analysis.* He would like to thank Pamela L. Reed for research assistance on his essay and James A. Schear for his critique of an earlier draft.

**Selig S. Harrison** (Co-Editor) has been a Senior Associate of the Carnegie Endowment for International Peace since 1974 and is director of its program on Japan's Role in International Security Affairs. A former foreign correspondent for *The Washington Post,* he served as Northeast Asia Bureau Chief from 1968 to 1972. He is a former Senior Fellow in Charge of Asian Studies at the Brookings Institution and is the author of five books on Asian affairs, including *The Widening Gulf: Asian Nationalism and American Policy,* and co-author with Diego Cordovez of *Out of Afghanistan: The Inside Story of the Soviet Withdrawal.*

**John D. Isaacs** has served as President and Executive Director of the Council for a Liveable World since 1991 and previously served as its Legislative Director from 1978 to 1990. He was the principal foreign affairs legislative assistant to former Representative Stephen J. Solarz (D-NY) from 1975 to 1977. He has served as a monthly contributor to and editor of *The Bulletin of the Atomic Scientists* and co-author of *Preventing a Biological Arms Race.*

**Edward C. Luck** served as President of the United Nations Association from 1984 to 1994 and is currently President Emeritus and Senior Policy Advisor. He previously served as Executive Vice

President and Vice President for Research and Policy Studies of the Association. He has edited two books and has contributed to *Foreign Policy, Current History,* and other journals.

**Masashi Nishihara** (Co-Editor) is Professor of International Relations at the National Defense Academy and Director of the First Research Department at the National Institute for Defense Studies. The views expressed in this book are entirely the author's and do not necessarily represent those of the Japan Defense Agency. Professor Nishihara has a law degree from Kyoto University and earned a Ph.D. in Political Science from the University of Michigan. He is the author of *East Asian Security and the Trilateral Countries* and co-author of *Keeping the Peace in the Post–Cold War Era: Strengthening Multilateral Peacekeeping* (Trilateral Commission Report No. 5, 1993).

**Steven Ratner** is an Assistant Professor of Law at the University of Texas. He has served in the Office of the Legal Adviser, U.S. Department of State, and as a legal advisor to the U.S. delegation at the Paris Conference on Cambodia. He is the author of a 1994 Council on Foreign Relations book, *The New U.N. Peacekeeping: Building Peace in Lands of Conflict After the Cold War.* Portions of his essay in this book appear in the Council study.

**Akihiko Tanaka** is Associate Professor of International Politics at the Institute of Oriental Culture, University of Tokyo. He received a Ph.D. from Massachusetts Institute of Technology in 1981 and has served as a member of the Japanese Government's Economic Advisory Council and Industrial Structure Council. He is the author of *The World System* and *Sino-Japanese Relations 1945–1990.*

**Takako Ueta** is Associate Professor of International Studies at International Christian University. She has served as a Special Adviser to the Japanese Embassy in Belgium in charge of NATO and European security issues and as a member of the Japanese delegation to the Stockholm Council of the Conference on Security and Cooperation in Europe. She is the author of *The Development of the Regional Security System Under the League of Nations* and co-author of *The CSCE 1975–1992.*

# CARNEGIE ENDOWMENT FOR INTERNATIONAL PEACE

The Carnegie Endowment for International Peace was established in 1910 in Washington, D.C., with a gift from Andrew Carnegie. As a tax-exempt operating (not grant-making) foundation, the Endowment conducts programs of research, discussion, publication, and education in international affairs and U.S. foreign policy. The Endowment publishes the quarterly magazine, *Foreign Policy*.

Carnegie's Senior and resident associates—whose backgrounds include government, journalism, law, academia, and public affairs—bring to their work substantial first-hand experience in foreign policy through writing, public and media appearances, study groups, and conferences. Carnegie associates seek to invigorate and extend both expert and public discussion on a wide range of international issues, including worldwide migration, non-proliferation, regional conflicts, multilateralism, democracy-building, and the use of force. The Endowment also engages in and encourages projects designed to foster innovative contributions in international affairs.

In 1993, the Carnegie Endowment opened the Center for Russian and Eurasian Studies in Moscow. Through joint projects on issues of common interest, Carnegie associates and researchers at the Moscow Center are working with Washington-based Carnegie associates to enrich intellectual and policy debate in the United States as well as in Russia and other post-Soviet states.

The Endowment normally does not take institutional positions on public policy issues. It supports its activities principally from its own resources, supplemented by nongovernmental, philanthropic grants.

Carnegie Endowment for International Peace
2400 N Street, N.W.
Washington, D.C. 20037
Tel.: (202)-862-7900
Fax: (202)-862-2610

# OTHER CARNEGIE BOOKS

The Carnegie Endowment books advertised in the following pages may be purchased from Carnegie's distributor, The Brookings Institution. A more complete listing of recent Carnegie books is available from Publications, Carnegie Endowment for International Peace, 2400 N Street, N.W., Washington, D.C. 20037, Tel. (202) 862-7900, Fax. (202) 862-2610.

To order Carnegie books, please contact:

The Brookings Institution
Department 029
Washington, D.C. 20041-0029
U.S.A.

Fax.(202)-797-6004
Tel. (202)-797-6258

Orders should be accompanied by a check or money order for the price of the book, plus 5.75% sales tax, plus $3.00 postage.

# THE UNITED STATES, JAPAN, AND THE FUTURE OF NUCLEAR WEAPONS

Report of the U.S.-Japan Study Group on Arms Control and Non-Proliferation After the Cold War

After a year-long examination, a high-level Study Group of twelve American and twelve Japanese specialists presented this searching analysis of the key global and regional arms control and non-proliferation issues facing the United States, Japan, and the international community. The Central theme of the report is that proliferation can only be prevented if the existing nuclear powers accompany their non-proliferation efforts with parallel moves to reduce and eventually eliminate their nuclear weapons in accordance with Article 6 of the Non-Proliferation Treaty.

The Co-Chairmen of the Study Group were William Clark, Jr., former Assistant Secretary of State for East Asian and Pacific Affairs, and Ryukichi Imai, former Japanese Ambassador to the United Nations Disarmament Conference. The report was prepared by Study Group member Selig S. Harrison, Director of the Endowment's Program on Japan's Role in International Security Affairs and a former Asia Bureau Chief for *The Washington Post*.

**1995/192 pp./$12.95**
**ISBN 0-87003-060-4 (paper)**

Forthcoming:

# NUCLEAR POWER, NUCLEAR WEAPONS, AND JAPANESE POLICY

Selig S. Harrison, Editor

Japan's policy of basing its nuclear power on reprocessed plutonium has aroused widespread suspicion, especially in neighboring East Asian countries, that Japan is secretly planning to develop nuclear weapons. This book presents the views of a leading Japanese proponent of the reprocessing policy, Atsuyuki Suzuki, Professor of Nuclear Engineering at Tokyo University; a leading critic, Jinzaburo Takagi, Director of the Citizens Nuclear Information Center; and Tae-woo Kim, a South Korean specialist who warns that the Japanese nuclear program could lead Seoul to pursue a reprocessing capability of its own.

Ryukichi Imai, former Japanese Ambassador to the U.N. Disarmament Conference, discusses the plutonium policy in the context of Japan's approach to global and regional non-proliferation and nuclear arms control issues. The introductory essay by Selig S. Harrison, Director of the Endowment's Program on Japan's Role in International Security Affairs, analyzes the history of the domestic debate in Japan over the acquisition of nuclear weapons and assesses the possibility of a Japanese nuclear weapons program.

**December 1995/112 pp./$9.95**
**ISBN 0-87003-065-5 (paper)**

# INDIA & AMERICA AFTER THE COLD WAR

Report of the Carnegie Endowment Study Group on U.S–Indian Relations in a Changing International Environment

Selig S. Harrison and Geoffrey Kemp

Why have relations between India and the United States so often been troubled, and what can be done to improve them in the aftermath of the Cold War? Does India matter to the United States? Is India a "basket case," or is it emerging as a major economic and military power?

The Carnegie Endowment for International Peace invited 34 experts to conduct a structured examination of key issues likely to affect relations between Washington and New Delhi in the nineties. The Carnegie Study Group on U.S.-Indian Relations in a Changing International Environment, under the chairmanship of two former U.S. ambassadors to India, Harry G. Barnes, Jr., and Robert Goheen, included scholars, business leaders, U.S. officials, members of Congress, and others who shape relations between the world's two largest democracies. Based on deliberations beginning in May 1991, the Study Group's report presents recommendations to both gov: ernmnents on a wide range of issues, including nuclear and missile proliferation, South Asian arms control, U.S.-Indian military cooperation, trade and investment, the Kashmir dispute, and human rights abuses.

Authors Selig S. Harrison and Geoffrey Kemp, Senior Associates of the Carnegie Endowment and Co-Directors of the Study Group Project, are both veteran South Asia specialists. Harrison is the author of five books on Asia, including India: The Most Dangerous Decades, and a former South Asia Bureau Chief of The Washington Post. Kemp served as Special Assistant to the President for National Security Affairs and Senior Director for Near East and South Asian Affairs on the staff of the National Security Council. He is the author of The Control of the Middle East Arms Race.

1993/88pp./$8.95
ISBN 0-87003-028-0 (paper)